MODERNIZE
YOUR CAREER
SERIES

$18.95

MODERNIZE
Your Job Search Letters
Get Noticed ... Get Hired

MASTER RESUME WRITERS

Wendy Enelow &
Louise Kursmark

Modernize Your Job Search Letters
Get Noticed ... Get Hired

Copyright © 2017 by Wendy Enelow and Louise Kursmark

ISBN 978-0-9966803-3-2

EMERALD CAREER PUBLISHING

Publisher: Emerald Career Publishing
                2265 Walker Road
                Coleman Falls, VA 24536
                www.emeraldcareerpublishing.com
                800-881-9972

Cover & Interior Design: Deb Tremper, Six Penny Graphics
http://sixpennygraphics.com

Distributor: Cardinal Publishers Group
www.cardinalpub.com

Printed in the United States of America

CONTENTS

Introduction

Why an entire book about job search letters? It can't possibly be that complicated!

Why so many different types of letters? One would think that you could use the same letter every time you upload, email, or mail your resume.

What real purpose do job search letters serve? It seems as though no one reads them, so why bother?

The process of job search has become much more complex and competitive than in years past. To succeed, you must equip yourself with a portfolio of job search letters that will allow you to respond to different opportunities in a variety of ways: online, email, or good old-fashioned "snail mail." (Yes, "snail mail" can still work in certain situations!)

In ***Modernize Your Job Search Letters: Get Noticed … Get Hired,*** we begin with a chapter that outlines the strategies of effective job search letters. You'll find an in-depth discussion about the use of both traditional cover letters and modern-day e-notes—a more concise, yet very informative style of letter that can be used as an email message or uploaded along with your resume when responding to a job posting.

In Chapter 1 you'll also find information about other essential modern letter-writing techniques and the ever-increasing importance of keywords for Applicant Tracking Systems (the technology that scans resumes, letters, and other documents to identify essential skills and qualifications).

Following that very important chapter, we introduce you to the 8 essential types of job search letters:
- Job Posting Letters
- Cold Call Letters
- Recruiter Letters
- Networking Letters
- Referral Letters
- Thank-You Letters
- Letters for Challenging Job Search Situations
- Job Proposal Letters

You'll find a chapter about each type of letter, with detailed explanations as to what it is, why you need it, when you'll use it, and how to write it. In addition, each chapter includes 10–30 different samples of that type of letter that you can use for inspiration as you write your own letters.

While not every job seeker will need each type of letter, you'll certainly need a number of them, based on how you plan and manage your job search. Consider the following scenarios:

- **Responding to an online job posting:** You'll most likely use a modern e-note to briefly, yet powerfully, communicate your qualifications that align with the company's hiring requirements. Job response letters can include all types of information, ranging from specific work experiences to special projects and notable achievements to strong academic credentials—whatever will instantly resonate with the employer.

  Your e-note should convey a rich message of your value to that company for that specific position. And because it is short and to the point, it is quick and easy to read, an essential consideration for anyone who's hiring and has a multitude of candidate letters and resumes to review.

- **Writing to a recruiter:** You can use an e-note or a more standard cover letter. In fact, your letter can be quite similar to the one you would send to a company in response to a job posting, assuming you're contacting that recruiter for the same type of opportunity.

  However, often you will want to share information with a recruiter that you wouldn't initially share with a company—salary requirements, geographic preferences, special educational or health care needs for your children, and other more personal information.

- **Reaching out to your professional network:** The tone, style, and substance of a networking letter will generally be quite different from the other 2 letters just mentioned.

  You'll want to share your job objectives with your network contacts and remind them of the most notable experiences, achievements, or skill sets you have that relate to those objectives. Because you're writing to people you know, this letter is more informal. Your ultimate goal is to get referrals to their colleagues and contacts to further expand your network and uncover new opportunities.

- **Following up after an interview:** The candidates who get the job offers are often the people who know how to "play the job search game," and that means sending thank-you letters after every interview to each person that you met—in person or virtually.

  Well-written thank-you letters communicate that you're truly interested in the job opportunity and allow you to reiterate your most notable qualifications—the things that make you unique, memorable, and distinctive.

Most importantly, today's modern job search letters are customized to each opportunity, sharing compelling and memorable information—skills, achievements, experiences, credentials—to position you as a top candidate. It might be that some people won't read your letters, but for all of those who do, your career story is what will set you apart from—and ahead of—others vying for those same opportunities.

To provide you with the very best strategies and techniques to write powerful job search letters, we called on 50+ of our professional colleagues to contribute their letters to this book. With their contributions, you will enjoy a wide diversity of samples to help you write, format, and design powerful job search letters.

Be sure to use this book with its companion—***Modernize Your Resume: Get Noticed … Get Hired.*** With both books in your job search toolkit, you'll be well prepared to tackle the competitive world of job search, stand out from the crowd of other candidates, clearly communicate your value, and win the offer.

And that's our goal in writing this book: to give you the tools you need to differentiate yourself from other job seekers and succeed in landing the opportunities that you want.

How to Use This Book

We've structured this book to make it as easy as possible for you to find samples and information about the 8 distinct types of modern letters you'll need to effectively manage your job search campaign.

Chapter 1—a must-read for everyone—explores the concepts, strategies, and techniques for writing and formatting modern job search letters and e-notes. We outline critical considerations for developing and presenting content in the most modern method possible to enhance the chances that your letters will get noticed, be read, and result in interview opportunities.

In each of the next 8 chapters, you'll find detailed information on how to write and use each type of letter you'll need in your search. We discuss what you want to achieve with each letter, share ideas for content, and give you a solid understanding of what your audience wants and expects. Pay special attention to chapter 8 if you face a challenging situation—career change, military transition, post-incarceration, or a personal situation that may be a factor.

Along with our instruction, you'll find a rich portfolio of sample letters for each category. Use these samples as the foundation for writing and formatting your own job search letters. Once you've developed your own portfolio, you will be able to respond quickly and efficiently to any potential opportunity, whether a job posting, recruiter contact, network or referral outreach, or interview follow-up.

In the Resources section of this book are 2 valuable writing resources:
- List of 426 verbs to use in writing strong and actionable content.
- List of 221 personality descriptors and attributes to best portray your own capabilities using the strongest and most accurate language possible.

The final section, the Index, lets you search for sample letters based on a long list of industries, professions, and job search circumstances (e.g., career change, military transition, incarceration) so you can find letters that are most relevant to your career.

Our Commitment to You

If you follow our guiding principles for letter writing and formatting, and study the letter samples in all of the 8 categories, we promise that the job search letter development process will be easier, faster, and much more effective for you. You'll be able to write all of the powerful job search letters you need to help you *get noticed* and ultimately *get hired*.

CHAPTER 1:
Welcome to the World of Modern Job Search Letters

Are you ready to start building your portfolio of job search letters? They are an integral part of finding a new position, and you are likely to need multiple types of letters for different contacts and situations.

This book is your guide throughout the process. Just follow along as we share more than 125 sample letters and explain each of the 8 types of job search letters you'll need:

- Job Posting Letters
- Cold Call Letters
- Recruiter Letters
- Networking Letters
- Referral Letters
- Thank-You Letters
- Letters for Challenging Job Search Situations
- Job Proposal Letters

Not everyone will need all 8 types of letters, but we're certain you'll need at least 4 or 5!

Why Do Job Search Letters Matter?

The true value of job search letters is that they let you share *specific* information—achievements, project highlights, work experiences, educational credentials, and other qualifications—that relates directly to a job posting, recruiter search, networking contact, or referral.

More often than not, job seekers prepare a single resume to use for every opportunity. For the most part, that's fine. At times you'll want to customize your resume a bit for this job or that job, but the majority of the document remains the same.

That's why job search letters are so critical: **They are customized to each opportunity.** They bring to the forefront what matters most in each precise situation. Job search letters allow you to:

- **Showcase the most important items from your resume** that will best position you as a prime candidate for a specific opportunity. Your letters will bring to the forefront *that* information, *those* skills, *this* job experience—whatever is most valuable.

- **Go beyond your resume.** You might share details of a particular project, an industry that you know well, a customer market in which you have extensive contacts … a whole host of items that you might not have focused on in your resume because they aren't the highlights of your career. But in some cases, they may matter most.

- **Highlight details that you know will resonate** with your networking contacts—information that they can use to introduce you to their connections who might be looking for candidates with precisely your skills. Such information is valuable for both networking letters and referral letters to people with whom you want to build connections and explore opportunities.

- **Share information about your special circumstances**—career change, military transition, and other unique situations. More often than not, this type of information is not included in a resume, so your job search letter becomes the tool for sharing relevant details so that hiring managers, HR professionals, recruiters, and other decision makers understand your true career story.

> **Pro Tip: Share what's relevant for the specific situation.** How much information you share in a job search letter versus what you will wait to share in an interview will depend entirely on your career, your current goals, your challenges or obstacles, the company or recruiter you're approaching, and other specifics. You'll make an individual decision with each outreach.

Today's Modern Job Search Letter

What is a modern job search letter? What makes it different from letters of years past? What makes it special and unique?

> # 6 Hallmarks of a Modern Job Search Letter
> - **Instantly communicates why you're writing**
> - **Clearly establishes *who* you are**
> - **Captures attention by addressing your reader's needs and interests**
> - **Includes specific examples of value and success, not just generic qualifications**
> - **Is succinctly written and easily readable, appealing to human and electronic readers**
> - **Closes with a call to action**

To demonstrate the 6 hallmarks in action, let's take a close look at 6 job search letters. As you'll note from the accompanying text, many of the letters demonstrate multiple hallmarks, but we've chosen the most important and most impressive hallmark to showcase in each letter.

Hallmark #1: Instantly Communicates Why You're Writing (Example: Antonio Martinez)

We begin with Antonio Martinez, a senior operations manager looking to move into a higher-level management role. His letter (page 7) makes it instantly obvious why he's sending his letter and resume.

- The bolded subject line—*Global Operations Manager*—draws the reader's attention and leaves no doubt about the position for which he is applying.

Cover Letter

Antonio Martinez
Boston, MA 02115
617-727-6636 ▪ LinkedIn.com/in/antonio.j.martinez ▪ ajmartinez@gmail.com

March 22, 2017

Mr. Harold Venter
Chief Operations Executive
Amherst Logistics Corporation
1211 Pierce Street
Marlborough, MA 01752

Subject: Global Operations Manager

Dear Mr. Venter:

I am intrigued by your requirements for a Global Operations Manager because they match the major accomplishments of my career. I love the operations function—the people, logistics, and technology and the satisfaction from driving continual and measurable improvements in performance.

As my resume shows, I have established a record of success in multiple areas, including the following:

- **Revenue enhancement:** Applied multi-geography experience and cross-functional leadership to identify and execute measures that led to multimillion-dollar revenue results.

- **Leadership in a high-demand, stressful environment:** Played a critical role in increasing regional market share 27% while simultaneously reducing operating expenses 21%.

- **Change management:** Partnered with diverse groups and individuals at all levels of the organization to drive strategic change and innovative solutions that increased productivity at least 15% and profitability approximately 12%.

Currently, I am completing my MBA and investigating employment opportunities outside my present company. Based on my experience and my commitment to achieving excellence in all areas, I am confident I can bring measurable benefits to ALC as your Global Operations Manager and would like to arrange a meeting to discuss the opportunity. I'll follow up with you next week.

Sincerely,

Antonio Martinez

- In the first line of the first paragraph, again you'll see the words *Global Operations Manager* as he reiterates the position for which he would like to be considered. The rest of the first paragraph focuses on the depth of his experience in operations to further his candidacy.

Other notable components of this letter include the following:

- In the middle of the letter, 3 bulleted achievements showcase 3 areas of Antonio's expertise. Each contains quantified results—a great addition to any letter.

- The final paragraph starts with a quick yet important mention of his anticipated MBA, another strong qualification that positions him for higher-level opportunities and also explains why he's looking for a new career opportunity. He has advanced his credentials and he's ready to move up.

- The final sentence in the letter is his call to action, mentioning that he'll follow up next week to schedule an interview.

Hallmark #2: Clearly Establishes Who You Are (Example: Stewart Lester)

When you let your reader know who you are—your functional expertise and how you fit into the organization—you provide important context that makes it easier to understand your letter and, subsequently, your resume.

Stewart Lester's letter (page 9), our first example of an e-note, illustrates how to achieve both goals.

- The reader immediately learns who Stewart is from the first 2 bullets at the very top of his letter. He's a *Corporate Strategy Executive* and an *Investment Banker,* and he shares his 2 most notable achievements in each of these bullets. In an instant, his experience and value are clear to the reader.

- Stewart then connects those 2 points with a bold statement to the company, writing that he *can produce those same strong and sustainable results for you.*

- The following paragraph clearly communicates where and how Stewart fits into that specific position—EVP of Corporate Strategy & Development—with that particular company. He can do what the company needs: *perfect company strategy* and *design and implement external growth initiatives to realize that strategy.*

Notice how succinct this letter is: just 2 bullet points and 3 very short paragraphs. It is also an excellent example of Hallmark #5 (Is Succinctly Written and Easily Readable), which we'll discuss in just a few pages.

Hallmark #3: Captures Attention Instantly by Addressing Your Reader's Needs & Interests (Example: Patricia Crawford)

Patricia Crawford's letter (page 10) starts with an attention-getting 2-line headline in a shaded box at the top of the page:

HEALTHCARE MARKETING & SALES PROFESSIONAL
Developing Strategic, Consultative & Business-Building Solutions That Drive Revenue Growth

E-Note

From: **Stewart Lester,** slester999@gmail.com
Subject: **EVP—Corporate Strategy & Development** (LinkedIn Job Posting)
Date: May 13, 2017
To: **Michael Rich,** mrich@talentrecruiters.com

Mr. Rich—

- As a Corporate Strategy Executive for a Fortune 50, I helped build the most profitable company in its industry, delivering 5-fold growth in market value in just 5 years.

- As an Investment Banker with a top Wall Street firm, I led the design and execution of mergers, acquisitions, and other strategic transactions that delivered billions of dollars in shareholder value.

I can produce these same strong and sustainable results for your client.

I'm interested in working at a great company with talented people tackling complex issues—perfecting company strategy or designing and implementing external growth initiatives to realize that strategy. The EVP position seems to fit that description, and I would welcome your call to discuss the opportunity.

Stewart Lester
301-555-3826
slester999@gmail.com
LinkedInProfile

Resume attached as PDF

Cover Letter

PATRICIA CRAWFORD

Clarksville, TN 37040 ▪ 931.777.9311 ▪ patriciacrawford@yahoo.com ▪ http://www.linkedin.com/ patriciacrawford

HEALTHCARE MARKETING & SALES PROFESSIONAL
Developing Strategic, Consultative & Business-Building Solutions That Drive Revenue Growth

January 20, 2017

Joe Hanson
Managing Director
Oxford Recruiters, Inc.
8088 South End Street
Knoxville, TN 38009

Dear Mr. Hanson:

My strong qualifications for the **Sales Associate position with Eureka National Healthcare Associates** have prompted me to contact you. Most relevant to Eureka's requirements are the following highlights of my career:

☑ **Strong Sales and Closing Skills:** Record-setting close rate of 130 new accounts within one quarter.

☑ **Field Sales Background:** 11+ years of stellar sales performance, using expertise in product knowledge, a keen understanding of each client's needs, and an enthusiastic attitude in all of my client interactions.

☑ **Consistent Sales Goal Achievement:** Award-winning performance in regularly exceeding quotas for revenue, new client acquisition, and client retention—while steadily increasing sales goals.

☑ **Performance with Passion:** True compassion for the healthcare industry, medical community, and patients facing a myriad of debilitating and terminal illnesses.

I am available for positions spanning Nashville/Clarksville/Springfield/Ashland City, Tennessee, as well as communities near Hopkinsville, Kentucky. My compensation requirements are a minimum of $80K annually– preferably base plus commission—with a full benefits package.

I look forward to learning more about this interesting opportunity and can be reached at 931.777.9311 or via email at patriciacrawford@yahoo.com.

Sincerely,

Patricia Crawford
****
Attachment: Resume

Because she's applying to a recruiter for a Sales Associate position within the health care industry, Patricia's heading instantly addresses the company's specific needs as identified in the job posting. And, because this same shaded heading is used on her resume, she creates continuity between the 2 documents and clearly establishes her expertise and professional brand.

To be certain that her purpose is 100% clear, Patricia states the specific position and company name boldly in the first line. This clarity makes it easy for the recruiter to know why she's writing and to demonstrate that she meets the needs of the recruiter as well as the company.

Following are 4 short achievement statements that align directly with the requirements of the job posting: *sales and closing skills,* a *field sales background, consistent sales goal achievement,* and *performance with passion.* You'll see those specific qualifications—in bold—at the beginning of each of the 4 bullet points.

This is a great strategy! When the recruiter glances at the letter, those bold words—aligning perfectly with the job requirements—jump off the page. It couldn't be any clearer.

Because this letter is written to a recruiter, you'll note that the next-to-last paragraph shares geographic and compensation requirements that you would rarely include in a letter sent directly to a company. This information may be important to the recruiter to make the perfect candidate/company marriage.

> **Pro Tip: Share more to make a match.** When communicating with a recruiting firm, share information that will guide the firm in finding the right company match for you. Your professional and industry experience is essential, but you might also include more personal items—geography, compensation, citizen or immigration status, or special health care or educational needs.

Hallmark #4: Includes Specific Examples of Value & Success (Example: Richard Reynolds)

Although all of our 6 hallmarks are key to writing a modern job search letter, hallmark #4 is one of the most important—and one that all too many job seekers overlook.

Generic qualifications that could apply to anyone do little to position you as a leading candidate. Consider these qualifications for a typical sales representative: *selling, account management, price negotiations, customer service, and new product introduction.* Those skills are important—but they do little to differentiate one sales professional from another.

What's most important are specific examples of what you have achieved and the value you have delivered to the company by using those skills. Selling is a great skill, but *increasing sales by 12%–15% each year for 5 consecutive years* communicates a strong and precise message that is specific to an individual job seeker and aligns with the needs of the hiring company.

> **Pro Tip: Set yourself apart.** When you include specific and unique achievements, you immediately differentiate yourself from every other candidate … because no one else can cite those same results!

To demonstrate this hallmark in action, let's closely review Richard Reynolds's letter (page 13).

This is an example of a cold-call letter sent to a company even though there's no job posting. Richard has researched the company and knows that his experience, qualifications, and achievements are directly relevant to what a company like this one needs.

Here are the key elements of his letter that instantly communicate specific examples of his value and success:

- Read the first sentence … *Building high-performance logistics and distribution operations is my expertise.* In just 10 words (including 2 very important keywords: *logistics* and *distribution*), Richard states his true value to an organization. He then shares that he has achieved strong results for start-ups, turnarounds, and high-growth companies, making him valuable in just about any situation.

- The next section is the highlight of this letter: 3 single-line, bolded statements of specific career achievements and financial impact. These powerful indicators of his success are unique to Richard and thus distinguish him from all others.

- The following paragraph focuses on soft skills that are equally important in leadership roles and that have propelled many of his—and his team's—contributions.

- Then, back to his successes and contributions with 3 more bold, single-line statements of career and project highlights, along with specific, quantified accomplishments in logistics and distribution—precisely the opportunities he's interested in exploring.

- In the final paragraph, he shares that he's still employed. By including this statement—*Although secure in my current position*—Richard ups his value even further. He's the one looking to make a change and find a new challenge; he's not being asked to leave the company. Check another box in the value and success category!

One final note about Richard's letter: He has effectively used acronyms that are specific to the industries and companies he's targeting. Although you might not be familiar with UPH (units per hectare) or CPU (cost per unit), everyone in logistics and distribution will be, and that's what matters. He has positioned himself as an insider who knows the business deeply, and that's most definitely an additional value-add.

Hallmark #5: Is Succinctly Written & Easily Readable (Example: Chloe Bella)

In today's job search world, where so much of what we do is online, it is essential that you appeal to both human and electronic readers. What does that mean?

As Chloe Bella's letter (page 14) demonstrates, it means several critical things.

- Chloe begins by clearly identifying herself with a job title (*Non-Destructive Testing Technician*) that precisely matches the position she's applying for—thereby creating a perfect keyword match for electronic scanning.

- The letter is rich with acronyms, keywords, and industry-specific language: *UT, ET, RT, MPI, FPI*—terms that are vital to passing the electronic scan and conveying her expertise to human readers.

E-Note

From:	**Richard Reynolds,** richrey900@gmail.com
Subject:	Logistics & Distribution Operations Executive
Date:	March 23, 2017
To:	**Candace Osborn,** candace.osborn@masterlogistics.com

Building high-performance logistics and distribution operations is my expertise. Whether challenged to launch a start-up venture, lead a turnaround, or accelerate performance within a high-growth organization, I have consistently improved results:

- **Increased UPH as much as 48% and decreased CPU up to 24% year-over-year.**
- **Reduced operating costs more than $7M each year for 4 consecutive years.**
- **Improved net profitability 15% annually for multi-site logistics and distribution operations.**

I thrive in challenging, fast-paced organizations that require strong leadership with a "gentle hand," collaborating with employees, union officials, and executives to achieve aggressive goals. My teams will tell you that I've led successful employee outreach initiatives that strengthened communications and solidified each person's commitment to the company. Together, we have …

Excelled in leading new ventures from start-up through emerging growth into top performers:

- Transitioned 1.2M sq. ft. Greenfield operation from start-up to handling 1.3M+ units annually in first year.

Delivered unprecedented performance results:

- Sustained 99.9% inventory accuracy for X-CELLENT Studio Store's distribution center on 34M units annually while reducing operating costs $2M+.

Restored profitability to operations that were understaffed, poorly managed, and plagued by double-digit cost overrides:

- Captured $3M in savings within first year as Distribution Operations Manager for Tompkins Retail Group.

Although secure in my current position, I am confidentially exploring new professional opportunities and would welcome the chance to meet with you next week. I'll call to arrange a date and time. Thank you!

Richard Reynolds
~~~~~~~~~~~~~~
503-555-0274
richrey900@gmail.com
LinkedIn Profile
Resume Attached
~~~~~~~~~~~~~~~~~~

E-Note

From:	**Chloe Bella,** chloebella@yahoo.com
Subject:	**Non-Destructive Testing Technician**
Date:	March 22, 2017
To:	**Andrew Ribble,** ribbleandrew@testsolutions.com

I am a **well-qualified Non-Destructive Testing Technician with 11 years of experience** in several tightly regulated industries. My most notable qualifications include:

- Extensive knowledge of, and experience with, UT, ET, RT, MPI, and FPI testing methods.

- Certification as UT Level II, Nondestructive Test Inspector (Level II), and Fluorescence Penetrant Inspection (Levels I & II).

- Ability to quickly interpret complex technical documentation and achieve regulatory compliance.

- Proven success in prioritizing tasks and completing intense workloads under severe pressure to meet project deadlines, contractual obligations, and desired outcomes.

Further strengthening my credentials, I will be receiving my Bachelor of Science (BS) degree in Non-Destructive Testing & Engineering in May of this year.

My resume (uploaded per your instructions) provides further details of my credentials and accomplishments. I look forward to discussing the strong match between your requirements and my qualifications. Thank you.

Chloe Bella
808-555-1288
chloebella@yahoo.com

- Assuming that a relevant bachelor's degree is a job requirement, Chloe makes the wise decision to mention her upcoming graduation and lists the degree twice, both spelled out (*Bachelor of Science*) and abbreviated (BS), another tactic to be sure she passes the keyword scan.

- It is just as important that a job search letter engage human interest. Chloe's letter is definitely human-friendly, starting with the bolded statement in the very first line. She uses that valuable real estate to tell the reader what she does and for how long. With minimal effort and just a few words, she has shared what's most important at this initial stage in the interviewing and hiring process.

- This letter is very quick and easy to read. Paragraphs are short, sentences are just 1 or 2 lines, and there's plenty of white space to "breathe" between the paragraphs and bullets. In less than a minute, the reader learns Chloe's essential information and can move on to her resume for more details.

This job search letter meets all of the requirements for being succinct and readable by both electronic and human readers. Consider both as you write every letter.

> **Pro Tip: First, make the cut.** Particularly when responding to job postings, when you are likely to be one of dozens or even hundreds of candidates, you need to quickly and clearly establish that you have what the employer is looking for and distance yourself from the competition. When you get the opportunity to interview, you can share more ... but you must first get that opportunity!

Hallmark #6: Closes with a Call to Action (Example: Lisa Barnes)

Many job search letters end with a passive and clichéd expression—such as *"I look forward to hearing from you"*—that adds no value and does nothing to move things forward.

You can strengthen your letters by promising to follow up with a call, an email, or some other communication. Job search should never be a passive activity but, rather, a proactive effort to land a great new position. So don't just wait for others to reach out to you. Take control!

Read the last paragraph in Lisa Barnes's networking letter (page 16)—in particular, the last sentence, where she says, *I'll call next week to discuss further.*

Now Mr. Jones is expecting Lisa's call, and he doesn't have to make that call a to-do item for himself. When she does call as promised, he'll appreciate her professionalism and is likely to make time to chat.

> **Pro Tip: Keep the ball in your court.** Every time you write to an individual, the follow-up is under your control. You have that person's name, company name, and most likely an email address. If you don't have a phone number, you can call the main company number and ask for that person. Follow-up is courteous and professional and will make you stand out.
>
> In some cases, you won't be able to follow up. Let's say you've uploaded or emailed your letter and resume in response to a job posting, but no individual's name is given and the email address is impersonal (such as jobs@company.com). In those cases, don't promise follow-up in your letter. Just send it in—hope you might get lucky!—and move on to more productive job search activities.

Cover Letter

LISA BARNES

St. Charles, IL ✦ (773) 882-4456 ✦ lbarnes@gmail.com
https://www.linkedin.com/in/lbarnescpa

May 23, 2017

Herman Jones, Director of Profitability Analytics
Lighton Technology
2234 South Crescent Avenue
Des Plaines, IL 60068

Dear Herman:

We first connected at the EXCITE Conference in 2014 while I was with Woman-At-Work Corps. Since then, I transitioned to accounting and finance as a CPA and joined the midsized regional firm **Young & Smith** as a VP.

I am now seeking a role with more involvement in corporate strategy and financial management. As I investigate options, I request a meeting with you. Your historically thoughtful insights on career planning and management would be of great assistance as I consider a new direction.

As a former public accountant at **KPMG** with 15+ years in controllership, finance, and tax planning, I've influenced business strategy as a partner to operations, project management, and executive leadership. It's not simply about delivering data, but responding to changing markets with astute awareness of the financial implications of decisions, including:

↗ Persuading **10** partners to consider investment in a new outsourced accounting function that created **$550K** of new business.
↗ Redesigning tax prep around consistent, value-added best practices for **1K+** tax returns, saving FTE hours.
↗ Devising tax planning strategies for partnership revenue that limited liabilities related to a **$575M** investment.

These transactions, along with positions as a Board Member and Chair on nonprofits, allowed me to expand the traditional controller and CPA role and strategically advance operations. **I love these opportunities!** Fortunately, I worked for CFOs who saw my knack for strategic analysis and my forward-thinking mindset, giving me chances to step outside my role and take on more.

I've always admired your willingness to brainstorm on life and career. I trust you and hope we can connect soon to discuss my plans and your advice on how I should move ahead. I'll call next week to discuss further.

Best regards,

Lisa Barnes

Attachment: Resume

As we've seen in most of the letters we've just shared, Lisa Barnes's letter meets all or most of the hallmarks for a powerful, modern job search letter. Before closing with a call to action, Lisa's letter:

- Communicates why she's writing—to ask for help and thoughtful insights on career planning and management—and makes the network connection in the first sentence.

- Makes it very clear who she is—accounting and finance professional—in the second sentence.

- Follows with a short paragraph and 3 strong bullet points showcasing specific examples of her most notable achievements—the true value she brings to a new employer.

- Is relatively succinct in content and presentation. Although on the longer side for many of today's letters, it is written in short paragraphs and 1-line bullet points to enhance ease of readability.

The E-Note Versus the Cover Letter

As you reviewed the letters on the previous pages, you will have noticed that 3 of the 6 are formatted as email messages. They also tend to be shorter, easier to skim, and faster to read. These are the most modern of today's letters and what we refer to as **e-notes.**

When you are emailing your resume to a prospective employer, recruiter, or network contact, **your e-note is the email message.** There's no need for a separate email message stating you're giving them a letter; just give it to them immediately!

The other 3 letters are also modern in their content and overall presentation but are structured in a more traditional cover letter style. They're formatted with letterhead at the top—name and contact information—and look more like what you'd expect of a typical letter.

Both types of letters contain similar content, with just a few differences in how they are structured. Here's an overview.

	E-Note	**Cover Letter**
Follows all 6 hallmarks of the modern cover letter.	✓	✓
Is well written, easy to skim, and easy to read—no long, dense blocks of text.	✓ Tends to be shorter, with brief paragraphs and bullets that can be easily viewed on a mobile device or other small screen.	✓ May be a bit longer, but never more than 1 page and always structured for readability.
Gives readers essential information quickly.	✓ Tends to be direct and to the point, making the best use of valuable screen space.	✓ May be slightly more expansive, with a few more details and courtesies than the get-to-the-point e-note.

	E-Note	Cover Letter
Follows standard business letter format: letterhead, inside address, formal salutation, closing.		✓
Follows standard email format: subject line, salutation, signature block.	✓	
Uses appropriate language and tone.	✓ Although never too casual, an e-note tends to be less formal than a traditional business letter.	✓ Although never stuffy, a cover letter tends to take a businesslike and somewhat formal tone.

Pro Tip: E-notes and cover letters are interchangeable, for the most part, with just a few format adjustments required to convert from one to the other. Throughout this book we use the word "letter" to refer to both e-notes and cover letters.

Choosing the Best Letter Type

The obvious question to ask yourself is when to use an e-note and when to use a cover letter. As we've mentioned, e-notes tend to be shorter, but length is *not* the single determining factor. The easiest way to decide which type of letter to use is the method by which you're going to submit it. Consider the following situations to help you in choosing your letter type.

	Send E-Note	Send Cover Letter
Uploading your letter and resume in response to a job posting. • Carefully follow instructions from the job board, company, or recruiter for uploading your resume and letter. • If you can upload only 1 file, make your e-note or cover letter the first page and then follow with your resume. • Be sure that your letter addresses the specific requirements in the job posting. • Incorporate keywords into your letter to help your application pass the scanning systems used in electronic job search.	✓ An e-note works perfectly for today's electronic job search. There's no need for formality. What matters is strong, relevant, and engaging content.	✓ If a recruiter pulls your letter from the database, an attractive and distinctive cover letter format will be more visually appealing than a plain-text message.
Emailing your letter and resume in response to a job posting. • State the job posting in your subject line so your reader knows why you are writing. • Be sure that your letter addresses the specific requirements in the job posting.	✓ Always use an e-note so your essential information is instantly accessible.	

	Send E-Note	Send Cover Letter
Emailing your letter and resume to a network contact.	✓ This is a perfect situation for an e-note. You already know the person and can get right to the point.	
Emailing your letter and resume to a referral.	✓ In your subject line and the very first sentence of your e-note, mention the name of the person who referred you.	
Emailing to the President, CEO, Chairman of the Board, or other top executive.	✓ Writing to a top executive at a startup or young technology company, an e-note will strike the right contemporary note.	✓ For a very senior-level presentation, the cover letter works best because of its formality and more traditional presentation.
Submitting your letter and resume via snail mail—USPS, UPS, FEDEX, or another carrier.		✓ An attractive cover letter will send the right message—professional and a bit formal—in select situations when snail mail is the best strategy.

Pro Tip: Use PDFs to avoid file and format glitches. Whenever possible—whether uploading a file or emailing an attachment—use PDF instead of Word files, unless instructed otherwise. Because PDFs retain the format integrity of every document, you can be certain readers will view your letters and resumes exactly as you created them.

Designing and Structuring Your Letters

Whether you choose an e-note or a cover letter, you'll make your best impression by using the correct format. The guidelines below walk you through each of the letter formats, top to bottom.

Cover Letter Letterhead

As you peruse this book, you'll find dozens of examples of attractive letters with nicely designed letterhead. The very different designs share a few common elements—things you'll want to pay close attention to as you are designing your cover letters.

- Your heading should **match your resume** for a consistent, cohesive, professional image and brand—and to instantly connect your letter with your resume.

- You'll notice that some letters include headlines and taglines (branding statements)—as in Patricia Crawford's letter on page 10. These headlines **also match the resume** and are optional—but they certainly capture attention and further reinforce your identity and value.

- Use a **clear and professional email address.** Even if you use a shared or casual email (smithfamily@ yahoo.com or soxfan@gmail.com) for personal messages, for your job search you'll want something more formal and professional—ideally, just your name @ your email provider.

- Always add your **phone number**—preferably a cell number where you can be reached at all times.

- You **do not need to include your physical address,** although you might want to share general information about your location. See pages 23–24 for further discussion and recommendations.

Cover Letter Structure

Follow the standard structure for business letters. Specifically:

- Insert the **date** at the left margin a few lines below your letterhead.

- Two or 3 lines below the date, add the **inside address**—the name and address of the person you're writing to.

- Use a **formal salutation,** placed 2 lines below the inside address. Your salutation should include a title (Mr., Ms., or Dr.) and last name, followed by a colon (not a comma):
    - **Dear Mr. Brown:**
    - **Dear Ms. Allen:**
    - **Dear Dr. Abernathy:**
    - **Dear Jane:** *(Use the first name only when you already know the person you're writing to.)*

- Although not required, a **subject line** allows you to immediately state why you're writing and eliminates the need for a wordy opening paragraph—you can jump right into your message. The subject line is placed 2 lines below the salutation and may be either left-justified or centered.

- Begin the **body of your letter** 2 lines below the salutation or subject line.

- Use **paragraphs and/or bullet points** to convey your cover letter information. Keep the letter readable by limiting any text to 3 or 4 lines maximum.

- Consider adding a **graphic—a graph, table, logo, shaded box, or other appropriate image—**as an attention-getting element, provided it adds value and is relevant to your message.

- End your letter with a **complimentary close** such as "Sincerely," "Cordially," or "Very truly yours."

- Leave 2 or 3 blank lines and then **type your name.** You might like to include a scanned signature or a script signature above your name, although it's not necessary. If you're snail-mailing the letter, sign your name on the hard copy.

- Another optional element is an **enclosure or attachment notation** below your name, indicating that you are also sending your resume.

E-Note Structure

You can instantly identify the e-notes in this book because they look like email messages, and they lack the visual design elements that you will find in the cover letters. And that's okay! As noted in the previous chart, e-notes tend to be direct and to the point; the message is what counts.

Still, e-notes have their own formatting considerations:

- Pay attention to what's shown in the "from" field when you send an email. If yours is confusing or incomplete (e.g., "Jessica's Email" or "Dave K"), adjust your email settings so that **just your full name** is shown.

- Use a **professional-sounding email address**—ideally, your name @ your email provider.

- Think carefully about your **subject line.** Don't waste the opportunity to share valuable information about yourself in the subject line, before your message is even opened. Here are a few examples—and you'll find many others in the e-notes throughout this book.
    - **Account Manager**—5 straight years of exceeding sales goals *(Share something impressive that will make the recipient want to open your email.)*
    - **Referred by Adam McKinsey** *(A referral is always your strongest possible introduction.)*
    - **Mechanical Engineer/Automotive**—Indeed.com posting—GM, Nissan, Toyota experience *(Let your reader know why you're writing and something that will set you apart from others.)*

- Begin your e-note with a **salutation** that is appropriate for email, perhaps less formal than a cover letter. For example:
    - **Ms. Sanders—** *(Writing to someone you don't know or don't know well.)*
    - **Dear Mr. Blackthorne,** *(Notice that these salutations are followed by a comma or dash, not the formal colon of a cover letter.)*
    - **Hi John** or **Hey John,** *(Writing to someone you know well.)*
    - **No salutation**—simply begin your letter *(Writing to an anonymous email address provided in a job posting and not to an individual.)*

- Write the content of your letter in **short paragraphs** and/or **short bullet points.** Pay close attention to the density of each block of text. You want your e-note to be crisp, airy, and easily skimmed.

- We recommend that you use a **complimentary close** (such as "Sincerely," "Best regards," or "Cordially"), but it's optional.

- Create a professional **signature block** that you use on *all* of your email correspondence. Not only is it professional, it makes it easy for readers to contact you or learn more about you with a single click. Your signature block should include:
    - Your name.
    - One phone number, ideally a cell phone so you can be reached at any time. Consider adding "call or text" if you are open to receiving text messages from contacts and employers.
    - Your email address, live-linked for instant connection.
    - *Optional but recommended:* your LinkedIn profile URL, again live-linked.

- *Optional*: your address or general location. See pages 23–24 for discussion and recommendations.
- *Optional; include as appropriate to you:* your Twitter handle, personal website, social media addresses, and other relevant links.

> **Pro Tip: Use both e-notes and cover letters for inspiration.** Any of the letters in this book can be switched from one type of letter to another—from e-note to cover letter or cover letter to e-note. We included a good variety of both types to give you lots of samples to choose from to meet your unique job search requirements.
>
> If you like the style and content of one of the samples, use it as a model and adapt as needed for your specific circumstances and for the type of letter that you're sending.

Job Search Letters & Applicant Tracking Systems

As you probably know, Applicant Tracking Systems (ATS)—also known as keyword scanning systems—are the backbone for electronic scanning of resumes, letters, and other job search communications. What does that mean to you?

Just like your resume, your job search letters must be rich with the keywords that reflect the industries and professions you are targeting. Every time you upload a letter, it will most likely be scanned by the same ATS as your resume. In your letter, be sure to integrate keywords that you know will resonate with an employer. Work them naturally into the text of the letter.

For example, note the keywords in the text samples below. We've <u>underlined</u> them so you can easily spot them.

- Directed <u>recruitment</u>, <u>staffing</u>, <u>manpower planning</u>, and <u>training</u> programs for IBM's 2000-employee customer service division. *(Ideal for someone in human resources.)*

- Created a <u>fully integrated supply chain</u>, <u>distribution</u>, and <u>logistics</u> organization responsive to the company's needs as we expanded our <u>production</u> and <u>warehousing</u> operations around the world. *(Ideal for a production or operations manager.)*

- Spearheaded <u>design</u>, <u>development</u>, <u>implementation</u>, <u>troubleshooting</u>, and <u>end-user support</u> for new $3M <u>technology application</u>. *(Ideal for a software engineer, systems engineer, and others in technology development.)*

The most important thing to remember is to use keywords relevant to the industry and profession you are targeting—which may or may not be reflective of your past experience. If it is, great—that makes letter writing (and resume writing) so much easier. If not, try to uncover keywords that translate from your past experience to your current goals.

A particularly effective trick to get the right keywords into your letter and resume is to note that you're "qualified for" positions in <u>sales</u>, <u>product management</u>, <u>territory management</u>, and <u>new product launch</u>. When you use that terminology, you're being 100% honest in your content yet still able to pass the keyword scan and, hopefully, have your resume read by a human being.

Pro Tip: No need to mention that your skills are "transferrable." That instantly communicates a message that you're out of the industry or profession you are targeting and need to "transfer in." Why draw attention to that fact when you already "own" those skills and keywords?

Linkability

We've already mentioned that you should include live links in your letters to make it easy for a reader to contact you or learn more about you—we call it the "1-click, live-link rule." Consider these scenarios to understand the importance of this concept of linkability.

- A prospective employer reads your letter and wants to contact you to schedule an interview. With a single click of your live link, an email message pops up with your address already in the "To" field. Couldn't be easier!

- After reading your e-note, a recruiter wants to know more about you. One click opens your attached resume and gives her all the relevant details of your experience, education, and other qualifications.

- A network contact wants to have more information—beyond just your resume—about your career before introducing you to a colleague. Make it easy for him by including a live link to your LinkedIn profile. If well written, your profile will share new information about you and your career to supplement what he already knows. Plus, once on your LinkedIn page, he can look at videos, PowerPoint presentations, and any other electronic media you've included.

  LinkedIn has established itself as the leader in online job search. But depending on your level of experience, profession, and industry, other social media sites might also be valuable in your search.

  If you're a graphic designer with an exceptional presence on Pinterest, include a live link to that site. If you're a videographer, add a live link to a portfolio of your work that you've posted on YouTube or Vimeo. It might even be that your Twitter stream is filled with information that's on-point for a particular opportunity. Bottom line, share live social media links that are relevant to your career and not overly personal in nature.

- Increasing day by day are the number of people who have their own individual websites. Your site might include information about your career, achievements, project highlights, client engagements, or some of the multimedia items we just mentioned. If you have a website and it aligns with your job search, be certain to list it with a live link in your job search letters.

Pro Tip: Hyperlink. Live links to email, LinkedIn profiles, other social media channels, and websites are a must in both your job search letters and your resume. Give yourself a competitive advantage by making it easy and fast for people to connect with you and learn more about you.

What Happened to Addresses?

In years past, job seekers almost always included their addresses on their resumes, letters, and other communications. Today's modern resumes and letters do *not* have addresses. Your phone number and email address provide all the information that recruiters and employers need to connect with you.

Still, you might have good reason to include *some* geographic information. These guidelines will help.

- If you are pursuing opportunities only in the same area where you currently live, **list your city, state, and possibly your zip code.** Those 3 items are frequently used by companies and recruiters in their keyword scans to identify local candidates.

- If you live in a large metropolitan region and are willing to consider opportunities throughout that wider region, **include your general area:** *New York City Metro* or *Chicagoland Area* or *Silicon Valley Region.* You'll pass the keyword scan by using the city and/or region. Don't make your geography so tight (as in the previous bullet) that you're excluded from consideration.

- Speaking of exclusion, if your job search is not limited geographically and/or you're willing to look at lots of different regions, then **simply include your phone number and email address.** That's all the information anyone needs to contact you.

You'll see examples of all 3 of these approaches in the letters in this book, along with a wide variety of ways to format and present that information. Choose the information and the presentation that are best given your circumstances and the specific opportunities you are targeting.

Modernizing Your Resume

If you haven't yet modernized your resume, you'll be inspired to do so after you've learned how to modernize your job search letters. We strongly recommend that you make the same commitment to your resume by reading *Modernize Your Resume: Get Noticed … Get Hired.* Cover letters, resumes, LinkedIn profiles, and other job search documents work in tandem with one another, and it's essential that all of your career communications be modernized and relevant for today's job search market.

For details about *Modernize Your Resume: Get Noticed … Get Hired,* visit emeraldcareerpublishing.com, Amazon, or your local bookstore. It's available in print and as an e-book.

CHAPTER 2:
Job Posting Letters

What Is a Job Posting Letter?

If you're like most job seekers, a job posting letter is the one you will use most often. In fact, you will use this type of letter **every time** you respond to a job posting or advertisement. It's up to you whether you send it as an e-note or an attached cover letter but, either way, send it … always.

Be sure that you take the time to read about e-notes and cover letters in Chapter 1. That information is essential for every other chapter in this book.

> **Pro Tip: Customize every job posting letter.** The job posting tells you precisely what the employer is looking for, so your letter should demonstrate that you have it! Read on to learn how.

What Do You Want to Achieve in Your Job Posting Letter?

Your #1 goal in a job posting letter is to convey that your skills and experiences are a near-perfect match with the posted qualifications. How you do that will vary from letter to letter, based on your writing style and on what you've chosen to showcase in each letter. There is no single formula nor template.

As you'll read in detail in the next section, what you write in each letter should quickly and effortlessly demonstrate that you're a qualified candidate worthy of close consideration. Think of your letter as the appetizer to you, the main course. You want to feed the reader a bit of really good information that whets the appetite for even more—your resume and, ultimately, a personal interview.

How Do You Write a Job Posting Letter?

Writing a job posting letter can be easier than just about any other type of job search letter. Why? Because each job posting states precisely what the company or recruiter is looking for in a qualified candidate. So your task is straightforward … to demonstrate that you have exactly the skills and experience called for.

Because every job posting is different, each of your letters should be customized to the specific opportunity. Generic cover letters that simply announce you're applying for a certain position are largely ineffective. They're not worth the employer's time to read, because they say nothing that is unique or pertinent. Relevant details of your experience are what will attract employers and recruiters to you.

Your job posting letters must be:

- **Customized to each specific job posting,** allowing you to change the content of your letter to match each employer's or recruiter's needs. Your custom content might include specific skills and qualifications, job experience, training and education, language fluency, technology expertise … a whole host of items that you believe will be to your advantage based on the job, the company, and the industry—and as clearly stated in the job posting.

- **Memorable and distinctive.** Consider this: Most applicants responding to a job posting will have similar skill sets. Ask yourself what makes you unique … what you've achieved that others in your profession have not … what makes you most memorable and distinctive.

  Highlight that distinctive information so that your letter is more than just a list of skills. Not only will you distinguish yourself from others, you'll be interesting and memorable—a wonderful thing in job search!

- **Rich with keywords** that will resonate with a hiring company and recruiter. Keywords fall into a number of categories, and most will be important in every letter that you write.

  Consider the manufacturing manager applying for a higher-level position. He will want to include keywords that represent **hard skills** (e.g., production operations, quality assurance, materials management, union negotiations), **soft skills and attributes** (e.g., productivity improvement, team leadership, communications, organization), **employment details** (e.g., job titles, employer names, cities, states), and **educational credentials** (e.g., degrees, college and university names, professional and technical certifications).

  Similarly, when writing your letter you'll want to consider keywords in all categories to fully express how well you match a posted opening in every area the employer deems important.

- **Written to give you a competitive edge** over others vying for the same opportunity. Accomplish this by demonstrating your professionalism in how you manage your job search and by sharing interesting and memorable information that clearly positions you as a qualified candidate.

> **Pro Tip: Sometimes a tweak is enough.** We've just told you to customize every job posting letter—and that's great advice! But if you're applying to substantially similar jobs, you'll find that you can use substantially the same letter, with just a few tweaks to create a near-perfect match with the posting. Do take the time to customize, but don't think you need to start from scratch with every letter.

One final, critical thing to remember when writing your letters, your resume, and all of your job search communications is that you can never lie or misrepresent yourself, your skills, your qualifications, or your experiences. A misstatement or falsehood can cost you an interview, an opportunity, or even a job after you've been hired.

How Do You Submit a Job Posting Letter?

As instructed in each advertisement, you can submit a job posting letter in 2 different ways:

- **Upload your letter** along with your resume. Sometimes you will upload these documents as a combined file (letter and resume) and other times as 2 separate files. Make that decision based on the specific upload requirements for each posting.

  The upload instructions will tell you which file formats are acceptable, typically Word and/or PDF. We recommend that you use PDF, if you have that option, because it retains the integrity of your formatted documents.

- **Email your letter** along with your resume. Paste your letter into the body of the email message to create an e-note, today's most modern type of job search letter, as you read in Chapter 1. Then, attach your resume as a PDF (recommended) or Word document.

  Sometimes the hiring company or recruiter will give you specific instructions for how to email your documents, and it's essential that you submit as requested.

> **Pro Tip: Always send a cover letter, even if one is not required.** Some job postings will indicate that a cover letter is optional; others may not even mention a cover letter. Unless the posting tells you specifically *not* to send a letter, we strongly recommend that you give yourself an immediate advantage over other candidates with a letter that clearly communicates your skills and experience as they relate directly to that job.

Who Is the Audience?

In the previous paragraph, we mentioned both hiring companies and recruiters. It's important to understand that you'll be responding to job postings from both audiences. More often than not, your letters will be quite similar, showcasing the skills, qualifications, achievements, educational credentials, and other highlights of your career that relate most specifically to that job posting.

However, when writing to a recruiter, you might choose to share additional information that you would almost never share with a company at this initial point of contact. That information might include:

- Salary requirements
- Salary and full compensation history
- Geographic requirements
- Special family needs for health care, education, and other services
- Specific dates for availability to start a new job
- Personal information that will give the recruiter a broader perception of who you are

Whenever you're responding to a recruiter job posting, be sure to follow the letter-writing techniques in this chapter *and* in Chapter 4, where we share letters written specifically for recruiters—letters that demonstrate the bulleted items we just listed and other special considerations.

To Whom Do You Send It?

The answer to this question depends on the instructions in the specific job posting. Either you'll upload your letter to the company's website, in which case you'll address it to the department or person indicated, or you'll send it via email. We've discussed both of these methods in the previous few pages.

In many instances no one person or single department will be mentioned and, therefore, you don't need to address it to anyone.

> **PRO TIP: If the job posting does not state to whom you should submit your information, omit the salutation line altogether.** Do not use "To Whom It May Concern," "Dear Sir/Madam," "Dear Hiring Manager," or any other generic language. Those introductions are dated and no longer necessary.

If no name is provided, we think it's worth a little effort to try to find one. When you do that, you'll accomplish 2 things:

- **You'll have a specific individual with whom to follow up.** Although you're not guaranteed to get a response from phone and email follow-up, it is certainly worth the effort. If you're able to connect, you will have set yourself apart from other candidates and gotten the attention of someone in the company or recruiting firm. In fact, the extra effort—when successful—may get your letter and resume "pulled from the pile" and put on top of the desk!

- **You'll demonstrate that you went the extra step and did your research,** sending a strong message about your capabilities and your commitment to that company.

The best places to find people's names—and often their direct contact information—are on the company's website, the company's LinkedIn or Facebook page, an individual's LinkedIn profile, or another online networking site such as about.me or XING. It's amazing the type of information you can find with just a bit of effort. Put it forth!

What Are the Unique Characteristics of a Job Posting Letter?

On the following pages you'll find 30 professionally written job posting letters. Each one demonstrates good writing, effective design, and content that's carefully targeted for a specific position.

The 30 letters are divided into 3 groups:

- 10 Job Posting Letters for College Graduates, Young Professionals, and Entry-Level Workers (pages 29–38)
- 10 Job Posting Letters for Mid-Career Professionals (pages 39–48)
- 10 Job Posting Letters for Experienced Professionals, Managers, and Executives (pages 49–58)

In a box at the bottom of each letter, you'll find a few short notes about why the letter was written the way that it was, the most important elements of that letter, and other strategic insights.

From:	**James Malak,** jakemalak@gmail.com
Subject:	**Accounting/Finance Co-op, PA Location**
Date:	May 13, 2017
To:	**Loretta Campbell,** loretta.campbell@jnj.com

Ms. Campbell,

As a rising 3rd-year Finance/Accounting honors student in Drexel's 5-year, 3-co-op program, I am very interested in Johnson & Johnson's 6-month co-op position beginning this Fall. I am confident that my leadership activities, strong work ethic, and previous co-op work have prepared me well for this opportunity. I hope you will consider me a competent, motivated, and viable candidate.

Recently I completed my first co-op as a Financial Reporting & Analysis intern at a global chemical company that is on target to reach $1B in net sales across 19 countries. Working for a large enterprise with such expansive reach was an eye-opening experience for me that cultivated a genuine interest in international business.

I hope to build on this momentum and accelerate my leadership potential through a J&J co-op. And, upon graduation (in 2020), my aspiration is to gain acceptance into your esteemed 2-year Finance Leadership Development Program (FLDP), where I can continue building the necessary knowledge and skills required of an effective leader.

My resume is attached. In addition to my co-op and academic credentials, you will note that I am the recipient of 2 merit-based academic scholarships and an active member in several student-run organizations, including Alpha Beta Kappa—where I serve as elected Assistant Treasurer.

I look forward to discussing my qualifications and potential contributions to the J&J brand. In the words of the FLDP, *The world is waiting … (I'm ready to) get started!*

Sincerely,

Jake Malak
****

James R. Malak
jakemalak@gmail.com | 502-337-7303
www.linkedin.com/in/jakemalak

Written specifically for a co-op position at 1 company, this letter opens by mentioning a leadership development program at Johnson & Johnson and closes with a quote from that program—thereby positioning this student as a promising candidate for both *current* and *future* career opportunities at J&J.

Kate Madden, MBA, CPRW • Fresh Start Resumes, LLC • www.freshstartresumes.com

JESSIE STONEWOOD

San Diego, CA 92130 ◆ LinkedIn.com/in/JessieStonewood
(619) 555-3278 ◆ JessieStonewood@gmail.com

June 3, 2017

Jean Marsden
HR Manager
Circus Communications
4545 Cycle Road
San Diego, CA 92122

Re: PR Assistant, Job#R28546

Dear Ms. Marsden:

I am a Communications college graduate and I am excited to start my new career as a professional. I really appreciate the time you have taken to view my resume.

Though I am fresh in the field I chose, I do have experience from an internship I completed with a PR firm in Beverly Hills. In that short time, I gained valuable marketing and communication skills that will make me immediately useful to Circus Communications as your PR Assistant. I am ready to help you from day one ... and eager to learn more.

Here are a few reasons why I am a great candidate for this position. I am ...

❖ **Very adept at using today's necessary marketing and social media tools,** such as Twitter, Facebook, Instagram, and WordPress.

❖ **Confident and well-practiced in both my verbal and written communication skills**. I know that if used wisely, words can be powerful drivers.

❖ **Comfortable communicating one-on-one with all levels of professionals,** so you can trust me when speaking to or emailing your clients.

❖ **Capable of learning new skills and applications quickly and proactively.** I will always be absorbing and building my expertise so I can become even more valuable to you.

I am available to interview anytime and look forward to learning more about Circus Communications. Thank you.

Sincerely,

Jessie Stonewood

Presenting herself as a smart, rising young PR professional, this job seeker emphasizes her current and future value to the employer. Her letter is enthusiastic, mentions a pertinent internship, and effectively outlines 4 skill sets most relevant to her new company.

Kate Boyle, CPRW • Ambition Resumes • ambitionresumes.com

TANYA BURDICK

Pleasonton, MO 64114

816.372.3551   tdburdick54@gmail.com

March 6, 2017

Mr. Lee Tonga
Tonga Design
2324 Elmwood
Lee Valley, MO 64081

Dear Mr. Tonga:

Re: **Designer—JustHired Listing**

I was excited to learn about your need for a designer. My skills, natural talent, and robust academic background would be a tremendous benefit for you in executing projects and delighting clients.

Let me point out three substantial reasons to consider me for the position:

Your Needs	*My Skills and Achievements*
Media Variety Experience	I designed and launched a **full branding concept** for a home staging business using a variety of **digital and print media** to produce a website, brochures, business cards, and labels within a three-week period. My customer was delighted with both the product quality and expedient turnaround time.
Knock-Your-Socks-Off Visual Communication Skills	I created the **winning design** for the Lee Valley University Dean's holiday card, beating out 12 other advanced-level graphic design student contestants, including two graduate students.
Self-Motivation & Positive Attitude	I believe you create your own opportunities. With graduation pending in May, I have already secured a **signed client contract** for a logo rebrand of a local gardening business.

I know I can deliver results for Tonga Design, and I would welcome the opportunity to speak with you in more detail. I will call your office to follow up next week.

Sincerely,

Tanya Burdick

Attachment: Resume

An updated version of the "T-style" letter that has been used for years, this letter includes 3 specific achievements that will be highly relevant to this employer. The remaining content is crisp, clear, and to the point. Notice the assertive close, promising a follow-up phone call within a specific time frame.

Andrea Adamski, CPRW • Write for You Resumes • www.writeforyoukc.com

From:	Kristi Cunningham, kcunningham35@comcast.net
Subject:	**Your Craigslist post for a Customer Service Representative**
Date:	April 27, 2017
To:	Benjamin Stone, benstone@kitchenstuff.com

Dear Mr. Stone,

As a devoted customer of Kitchen Stuff, I am excited at the opportunity to bring my strong customer support skills to your company and your clients.

My expertise is providing superb, friendly customer service to all. I enjoy working in busy, fast-paced environments, and I build rapport easily with colleagues and customers with an engaging and professional communication style. I am particularly adept at meeting customers' needs in a prompt and courteous manner.

And, of course, my knowledge of your products and resources will bring added value to customer interactions.

I welcome the opportunity for a meeting to see how I can help Kitchen Stuff continue to thrive.

Kind Regards,

Kristi Cunningham
303-507-1410
kcunningham35@comcast.net

Attachment: Resume

Customized to the specific company, this letter creates an immediate connection with the hiring manager and uses personal knowledge of the company's products as a strong selling point. The letter gets right to the point yet communicates a lot of information in just a few quick paragraphs.

Heather Seiden • Jewish Family Service of Colorado • www.jewishfamilyservice.org

ANTHONY MICHAELS

(858) 214-8862 ◆ amichaels@gmail.com ◆ www.linkedin/in/amichaels ◆ Cleveland, OH 56871

June 8, 2017

Mr. Scott Minkin
Trader Joe's Regional Captain
14 Canal Street
Cleveland, OH 56871

Dear Captain Minkin:

I am the adventurous First Mate you are seeking to lead your Cleveland location!

Like Trader Joe's, I bring joy to people's lives with delicious food at great prices. A manager of a popular neighborhood restaurant for 5 years, I will not only fit into your unique and friendly store atmosphere, but also bring a BS in Finance to drive profitability while ensuring exceptional customer service.

Why should I be lucky enough to wear the Hawaiian shirt every day?

◆ **My passion is making people happy with creative, great-tasting, affordable food.**

As a restaurant manager, I learned how to cultivate customer loyalty. I built personal relationships with patrons to drive repeat business and customer satisfaction. In addition to creating a restaurant training program that reduced staff turnover by 25%, I built a sense of ownership and pride among employees.

◆ **I am a leader who thinks strategically and thrives on hands-on, physically active work.**

My versatile skill set and "can-do" attitude have resulted in increasing responsibilities during my tenure at the restaurant. In addition to overseeing smooth daily operations, I manage finances, run events and promotions, and develop marketing collateral. Previously, I completed a Whole Foods financial internship.

◆ **I know what it takes to be a "good neighbor" (and wouldn't have it any other way)!**

Consistent with Trader Joe's commitment to community service, as a neighborhood restaurant manager I initiated programs to give back. Through golf outings, free catering events, and drives that donated a percentage of restaurant sales, we generated more than $100,000 for Cleveland-based charities.

I look forward to learning more about your goals for the Cleveland location and discussing how I can contribute to Trader Joe's bright future. Thank you for your consideration.

Sincerely,

Anthony Michaels

Enclosure: Resume

At Trader Joe's, Regional Managers are known as "Captains," the store manager title is "First Mate," and staff wear Hawaiian shirts as their store uniform. This letter appeals precisely to that unique culture and clearly communicates the necessary skills and experience for the specific job at that distinct company.

Julie Wyckoff, M.Ed., CPRW • Custom Career Solutions • www.customcareersolutions.com

MARY J. MCGOVERN, NCC, LAPC

(234) 789-5476 | Mary.McGovern@outlook.net
North Star, AK

March 22, 2017

Dr. Jenny Charlton
Moving Boundaries, LLC
8875 Native Heritage Bypass
Fairbanks, AK 99707

RE: **Rural Outreach Team Life Counselor**

Dear Dr. Charlton:

Having recently obtained my Master's degree in Mental Health Counseling, I am exploring opportunities in the field of social services that allow me to make a difference—specifically, to improve the quality of life for children and adolescents in rural environments.

In reviewing the attached resume, you will find that I have pursued every opportunity to work with experienced social service professionals throughout the Anchorage area. Having worked with people of all ages and cultural backgrounds, I find that I connect with and most enjoy working with young people. That work is exciting, challenging, and very rewarding.

I love to travel, am in excellent physical shape, and look forward to discussing potential assignments—primarily as a member of your mobile outreach team. May we schedule a time to meet? I am eager to support your efforts in "Broadening Horizons."

Sincerely,

Mary McGovern

Enclosure: Resume

P.S.   I recently completed a variety of life support programs related to wilderness survival in the Arctic, offer extensive knowledge of Alaskan culture and wildlife, and maintain a network of professional resources developed through our family-owned and -operated land tour business.

Rather than stressing hard skills and qualifications (which are outlined in the resume), this jobseeker emphasizes a genuine commitment to the clients served and the mission of this organization. The letter closes with a P.S. that highlights even more value.

Lisa Parker, CERM, CPRW, CEIP • Professional Resume Presentations • www.parkercprw.com

From: **Rick Smith,** rsmith@email.com
Subject: **Marketing Associate Position**
Date: June 2, 2017
To: **John Martin,** john.martin@acme.com

Dear Mr. Martin,

I was very excited to read your company posting on Xavier's *eRecruiting* database. My background—particularly my website development experience at Coco Products—is an excellent match with your requirements.

During my internship at Coco, I became very proficient in deploying social media as a communication tool:

- I was commended for the creative marketing pieces I created and the ways I identified new target customers. When my suggested changes were implemented, we increased web-based orders 20% in the first month.

- In addition, I demonstrated excellent project coordination skills by developing an effective tracking system through which all team members were held accountable for their task completion.

- Finally, I devised an effective report-back format that kept management informed of how the new marketing approach was performing.

In short, my creativity, coupled with my project coordination skills, are proven assets that I can bring to ACME. My marketing studies at Xavier have really given me an excellent grounding from which your company can benefit.

My attached resume will give you a more detailed view of my accomplishments and work experience. I am eager to meet in person so that I can further elaborate on how my business degree and experience can be of benefit to the challenges ACME faces. I will call next week in hopes of scheduling a meeting.

Sincerely,

Richard M. Smith
>>>>>>>>>>>>>>>>>>
rsmith@email.com
937-482-2842 (call or text)

For this graduating student, a relevant internship provides strong and specific examples of work experience, project highlights, and accomplishments relevant to the job he's pursuing. By closing with a promise to call, he puts himself in the driver's seat—rather than simply waiting for Mr. Martin to call him.

SETH JOHNSON

202-840-6348 • linkedin.com/in/sethjohnson • sjohnson@gmail.com

June 4, 2017

Jack Rayson, Chief Operating Officer
Native Digital
5454 Maryland Ave, 2nd Floor
Washington, DC 20036

Re: Web Analytics Specialist, Job ID# ND4356

Dear Mr. Rayson:

Websites have the power to do more than just inform. When designed thoughtfully and with the right tools, they can inspire people to do more, or do better, or change. As a website analyst and digital marketer for the past two years, I have experienced first-hand how data metrics give developers a deeper insight into user behavior, and how that data can be used to optimize the users' website experience.

Your job announcement is clear on what you expect from your next Web Analytics Specialist. The following summarizes why I believe I am a well-matched candidate.

- I regularly use Google Analytics to optimize website layout, design, and SEO and am advanced in building custom dashboards and reports. I am also **Google Analytics certified.**

- I am experienced with tag management software, including Google Tag Manager and Ensighten Manage, and have deployed a number of different tags to add functionality to websites.

- Having worked for web analytics software developers Ensighten and Anametrix for the past two years, I have a strong understanding of web analytics. I am also **Master Web Analytics certified** and **Ensighten Manage certified.**

I am focused on creating website experiences that encourage engagement, drive brands, and support missions with data and analytics. I would be happy to share my past experience and learn how I can help you.

Sincerely,

Seth Johnson

This job seeker makes an immediate connection with Mr. Rayson by sharing his philosophy about website design—a business that greatly interests them both! The 3 bullet points include specific skills, certifications, and experiences that relate directly to the position as described in the job posting.

Kate Boyle, CPRW • Ambition Resumes • ambitionresumes.com

From: **James Kimble,** JamesKimble1@gmail.com

Subject: **EMT Basic—San Diego Location**

Date: June 5, 2017

To: **HRcontact@westernambulance.com**

Working as an EMT for the past 11 months has reinforced my passion for this field and defined the type of medical professional I am—a compassionate caregiver and natural leader.

To summarize my qualifications for the position of EMT Basic in your San Diego location, expanding on the details you will find in my resume:

- I am a senior EMT for basic life support for a company of 70+ EMTs, have logged 1600+ hours of experience, and have worked many back-to-back shifts that have non-stop calls.

- As the senior EMT, I am expected to be a leader-by-example. I must remain up-to-date on protocols and procedures and practice them so that I am always a positive and proper influence to junior staff.

- Organization and thoroughness are part of my daily routine. My unit is always well stocked and clean, my paperwork in order and complete, and my ambulance mechanically safe and reliable for transport.

- Maintaining a perfect service record is important to me. As of today, I have not had a single driving accident, dropped a patient, broken protocol, or missed a shift.

As an EMT, I know there are three priorities that must always be met—exceptional customer service, the highest quality in patient care, and consistently sound judgment. I am committed to upholding all of these standards and will make a valuable addition to your team.

Please contact me, as I look forward to interviewing for this opportunity.

Sincerely,

James Kimble

=====================

858-743-9824—Call or text

JamesKimble1@gmail.com

Resume attached

This e-note is an ideal combination of professional skills and personal qualifications. First, bullet points call attention to skills, experience, and intangible qualities that are essential to success as an EMT. Bookending these points are paragraphs that highlight the job seeker's passion for the job and his understanding of its importance.

Kate Boyle, CPRW • Ambition Resumes • ambitionresumes.com

From: **Jane Robinson,** jane.robinson@mac.com
Subject: **Meeting Manager for AWM – Indeed.com Posting**
Date: June 5, 2017
To: **JobPosting23244@Indeed.com**

I am excited to apply for the position of Meeting Manager and have uploaded my resume as requested in your posting.

For the past 3 years, I have worked as Associate Director of Meetings for a national trade association. In that capacity, I developed expertise in vendor negotiations and contracting, excellent supervisory skills, and the ability to handle both the day-to-day and strategic planning responsibilities of a meetings office.

I am aware of the critical role that meetings play in the work of associations and would enjoy using my skills to provide excellent and cost-effective meeting planning services for AWM.

When we meet, I will share with you the planning document I developed for every meeting I helped manage. It has become an essential tool in my office, used by rookie and experienced meeting planners alike. I believe it will be of value to AWM as well.

I look forward to meeting with you!

Sincerely,

JANE ROBINSON

777-555-1229
jane.robinson@mac.com

This letter offers a strong and concise introduction that instantly communicates core skills and essential keywords. Then, notice the fourth paragraph. It is a promise of value! Jane has developed a tool that has become a must-have in her current office, and she offers to share it with her new employer.

Paul Martin, NCC • Howard Community College • www.howardcc.edu

TOM ANDERSON

tomwanderson69@ymail.com

(404) 555-1212

Metro Atlanta, GA

Outside Sales: #1 in Area HVAC Sales for 10 Years

June 18, 2017

George Jones, CEO
Big Box Home Products
1 Peachtree Crossing
Atlanta, GA 30068

RE: Outside Sales Representative—Atlanta

Dear Mr. Jones:

For years, customers in Atlanta have trusted me with the 3rd or 4th largest purchase most folks ever make. Meeting their home improvement needs with honesty, effort, and loyalty kept them happy—and kept me **Number 1 in HVAC sales in Metro Atlanta.**

I would like to talk with you about your Outside Sales position with Big Box Home Products. Some specifics about my background and achievements:

❐ **Exceeded company sales goals every single year.**
❐ **Ranked #1 in Regional Sales** for Georgia Power and Georgia Gas from 2010 to 2016.
❐ **Ranked #1 in Area Sales for Carrier** Corporation from 2006 to 2010.
❐ **Earned a top-notch reputation** for high-quality home improvement solutions in the Atlanta area.

The enclosed resume details my experience and achievements. If you agree that I may be a good fit for Big Box Home Products, let's schedule a time to meet. I will follow up with you early next week by phone and look forward to the conversation.

Sincerely,

Tom Anderson

The letter format captures immediate attention with a bold and relevant headline at the top. The letter itself is short and powerful, highlighting exceptional achievements that demonstrate consistent success in sales, the #1 qualification for the advertised position. Note the assertive closing—entirely appropriate for a sales person.

Alexia Scott, CPRW • A Winning Resume • www.a-winning-resume.com

From:	**Liliana Lee,** LilYee@gmail.com
Subject:	**Regional Director of Sales (Requisition #54331)**
Date:	May 27, 2017
To:	**Zachary Leong,** zacharyleong@MidlandProducts.com

Mr. Leong:

During my 10+ years' rapid progression in sales and management, I have anchored award-winning teams that delivered unprecedented market expansion and explosive revenue growth.

In your search for a leader who will inspire and ignite *your* sales team, please consider a few of my career highlights:

- Profitably built and managed more than **$85M** in sales.
- Course-corrected a key region to achieve **top national sales ranking** after years of low performance.
- Led sales team to earn annual **President's Awards for 3 consecutive years**.
- Elevated major Fortune 500 customer loyalty scores **from 55% to 95%.**

A hallmark of my career has been regional and team transformation, and I look forward to discussing how I can further develop and execute my innovative strategies for growth at Leong Enterprises.

Sincerely,

Liliana Yee
==================
LilYee@gmail.com
650-309-6789

Resume attached in pdf format

This e-note gets right to the heart of the matter: the candidate's proven success in leading sales teams and delivering award-winning sales results. Achievements are specific, relevant, and highlighted in bold in 4 succinct, hard-hitting bullet points that align directly with the requirements of the job posting.

Emily Wong, MIM, ACRW, CPRW • Words of Distinction • www.wordsofdistinction.net

SUZANNE SMYTH

(568) 572-7241 ◆ 1 Meadow Road ◆ Cleveland, OH 45279 ◆ suzannesmyth@gmail.com

June 1, 2017

Ms. Patty Gable, Principal
Acorn Elementary School
12 Broadway
Cleveland, OH 45279

Dear Ms. Gable:

For more than a decade, I have enjoyed the privilege of engaging young children in the learning process through literature-based lessons, dramatic play, and multi-sensory exploration. I am excited by the prospect of bringing my experience and creative energy to Acorn Elementary School to fulfill your mission of nurturing the social, emotional, and cognitive development of each student.

What skills and attributes make me the best choice for your new kindergarten teacher?

◆ **An innate ability to connect with students and provide a safe and comforting environment.**

As a kindergarten teacher for 10 years, I patiently guide children in overcoming separation anxiety by being a present, stable source of support as they embrace independent experiences separate from their primary caregivers. Students become ready to have fun, interact, and grow.

◆ **A passion for sparking children's curiosity and a contagious lifelong love of learning.**

In addition to earning a BA in Elementary Education with a minor in Educational Psychology, I pursue ongoing opportunities for professional development and enjoy incorporating new ideas in my classroom. My science lesson plan won a 2015 Ohio Educational Excellence Award for integrating technology, learning styles, and multi-sensory activities.

◆ **A proven record of building valuable partnerships with parents and fellow educators.**

I understand the importance of working with parents and colleagues to benefit each child's well-being. I developed a staff and parent workshop adopted by 3 local schools to implement statewide curriculum initiatives and share educational resources with parents.

I welcome the opportunity to interview to discuss how we can work together to benefit the children of Acorn Elementary. Thank you for your consideration.

Sincerely,

Suzanne Smyth

Enclosure: Resume

Despite being relatively lengthy, this letter is well designed to make it readable, and the relevant content is sure to engage the reader. The heading graphic is distinctive and perfect for a kindergarten teacher.

Julie Wyckoff, M.Ed., CPRW • Custom Career Solutions • www.customcareersolutions.com

CARLY SMITH, B.Sc.

1014 Shaw Street, Oakville, ON N0N 1N0
905.505.0000 | carly.smith@newleaf.com | linkedin.com/in/carly.smith.me

January 17, 2017

Diane Hopper, Senior Recruiter
Search Partners
9601 Lakeshore Blvd. W.
Oakville, ON N0N 2L2

Re: Contact Centre Service Manager

Dear Ms. Harper:

Your client's search for a Contact Centre leader may be over! My career is rich in examples of proactive leadership, business-savvy ingenuity, future-focused initiatives, capacity-building partnerships ... I have developed a level of expertise in this sector that is second to none.

In fact, as Senior Manager of Operations with communication giant Evans Communications, I developed a reputation for restructuring ineffective processes and motivating unengaged staff to exceed productivity and performance expectations. Examples of successes include:

- **Surpassing escalation wait time metric goals**, improving from scores of less than 40 (goal was 75) to scores that consistently ranked above 80.
- **Reinvigorating corporate projects that had fallen behind or underachieved.** You will find examples of these on my resume.
- **Quintupling sales leads** and re-energizing a stagnant revenue-generating product.

At my best in a fast-paced environment, I am looking for an employer that values a relationship-building business expert who blends technical knowledge and people leadership for outstanding bottom-line results.

I invite your call to meet and discuss next steps. Thank you for your time.

Carly Smith

Encl: resume

*P.S. I would love to share the strategies that allowed me to **quintuple** sales leads.*

This letter beautifully balances *content, structure,* and *design* to create an inviting message that is sure to catch the recruiter's attention. Note the P.S. that promises something unique and valuable if the recruiter takes the time to meet with this candidate.

Stephanie Clark, BA, MRW, MCRS • New Leaf Resumes • www.newleafresumes.com

Tori Blackwood

406-667-4606 — TORI.M.BLACKWOOD@GMAIL.COM
LINKEDIN.COM/IN/TORIBLACKWOOD — BILLINGS, MONTANA

April 3, 2017

Seth Jones
Montana Restoration Services, LLC
14 Waywind Drive
Billings, MT 59001

Dear Mr. Jones:

Re: **Accountant/Bookkeeper Posting**

For the past 10 years I partnered to grow Middleton Restoration, a State Farm preferred contractor, from the ground up. I created all the books and accounting methods and monitored them closely as the company grew to a $10M success. It was sold successfully earlier this year.

I am now ready for my next accounting challenge with a new organization so I can help them discover ways to save time, money, and effort. This is why I am applying to Montana Restoration Services today for the Accountant/Bookkeeper dual role. I know that I am a perfect fit for this position!

A few highlights from my accounting and bookkeeping career thus far include:

- ❖ Reviewing the books to determine places to scale back, save money, or reduce insurance costs.
- ❖ Performing careful checks and balances on the books as the company broke thousands, hundreds of thousands, and then millions of dollars in revenue.
- ❖ Building exceptional relationships with employees; hiring and training a new bookkeeper.

In addition, I possess a Master of Science in Accounting and a Bachelor of Science in Finance. I continually look for new ways to improve my expertise and strengthen my educational credentials.

I look forward to hearing from you soon so we can better discuss how I can help your small business grow into a multimillion-dollar powerhouse. Thank you for your time and consideration.

Sincerely,

Tori Blackwood

The story of this candidate's prior position is compelling: She helped grow a small business into a $10M company that was successfully sold. Certainly that story will capture the interest of the employer. Notice how each paragraph and bullet point is tightly written to make the entire letter very easy to read.

Laura Gonzalez, ACRW, CPRW • Masterwork Resumes • www.masterworkresumes.com

MATTHEW LINDST

5615 NE 82ⁿᵈ Street
Kansas City, MO 64063
T: 816.453.7227
E: mlindst@yahoo.com

June 20, 2017

Mr. Robert Green
Top Flight Airlines
2237 W. Woodson St.
Kansas City, MO 64081

Dear Mr. Green:

Re: **Director of Scheduling and Crew Planning**

It is with great interest that I submit my resume for your consideration. Highlights of my qualifications, detailed in the attached resume, include:

- More than a decade of top-level airline operations and management experience controlling budgets of up to **$8M**; negotiating, administering, and arbitrating **labor contracts**; and ensuring adherence to all **FAA regulations** for major airlines *TransAtlantic*, *Blue Sky,* and *World Air*.

- Delivery of strong results from consistent data analysis and management—for example, **reducing crew pairing penalties** from **7.9% to 2.4%** and improving simulator and instructor utilization to **slash annual training costs 26%.**

- A reputation for **direct and decisive leadership** with the flexibility to report and respond to the constantly changing demands of the industry, staff, and customers.

- Unique understanding of frontline issues stemming from past **flight attendant** and airline **customer service representative** experience.

I look forward to speaking with you to discuss this opportunity and will call next week to request a meeting. Thank you for your time and attention.

Sincerely,

Matthew Lindst

Every bullet point in this letter highlights details and achievements that support Matthew's candidacy for the position. The letter is crisp and to the point and closes with promise to call—keeping the follow-up under Matthew's control. The attractive heading is distinctive and immediately catches the reader's eye.

Andrea Adamski, CPRW • Write for You Resumes • www.writeforyoukc.com

From: **Greta Reynolds,** gretareynolds@gmail.com
Subject: **Project Manager**
Date: January 6, 2017
To: **Cameron Tucker,** cameron@tuckerenterprises.com

Dear Mr. Tucker:

I can provide the multidisciplinary strength and agility to excel as a **Project Manager** at Tucker Enterprises.

As my resume indicates, I have successfully implemented and monitored key projects that span event planning and technical troubleshooting, with an eye on cutting costs. I look forward to unleashing that experience in a role that calls for someone who can easily pivot from one challenge to the next.

The following is a snapshot of what I offer your company:

- **Troubleshooting.** A common thread in all of my roles is identifying opportunities to cut costs and improve workflow. Collectively, I have saved my employers nearly **$90K** through software improvements, hardware replacements, and vendor renegotiations.

- **Event Management.** I have spearheaded large-scale meetings and events—including vendor negotiations, **$40K** budget oversight, and technical set-up—for more than **500** attendees.

- **Technology Upgrades.** I have a track record of jumping in to help orchestrate enterprise-wide IT projects, including a network installation and a SAP system migration.

- **Financial Analysis.** I have 15+ years' experience conducting budget and financial analyses that supported C-level decision-making and influenced business strategy.

I have positioned myself as a respected project leader by collaborating with team members and vendors to exceed the expectations of my internal and external customers. By fostering cohesive relationships through trust and reliability, I have won the support of not only upper management, but my peers as well.

If you are looking for someone who will deliver all projects on time and under budget while juggling multiple moving parts, I would welcome an opportunity to discuss the results Tucker Enterprises could expect from me.

Sincerely,

Greta Reynolds
415.269.0024 • gretareynolds@gmail.com
www.linkedin.com/in/gretareynolds

Each bullet point is introduced with a bold keyword that highlights a relevant skill needed for the position, and the details that follow are specific examples of how those skills were used and what results were delivered. While overall the e-note is somewhat lengthy, each paragraph is a quick read.

Emily Wong, MIM, ACRW, CPRW • Words of Distinction • www.wordsofdistinction.net

Sarah Nguyen

55 Southwest Lane, Airdrie, AB T1T 1T1 • 403.111.1111 • <u>spnguyen@mail.com</u>

Quality Assurance Analyst

Software Engineering Support • Testing & Programming • Defect Management

May 15, 2017

Ms. Amanda Borne
Chief Information Officer
Northern Communications Ltd.
14 Valley Boulevard SE
Calgary, AB T2T 2T2

RE: **Quality Assurance Analyst (Job Posting #13-2017B)**

As an IT Quality Assurance Analyst with **more than 15 years of experience** working in time-sensitive, high-pressure environments, I am confident I have the skills and qualifications it takes to contribute to your team.

Consider these highlights:

- An energetic team player for the past 4 years with Production Energy, Inc., I have a talent for **building relationships, performing a wide variety of tests, and preparing reports and documentation**.

- My professional style emphasizes **problem identification and issue resolution, and I always keep the big picture in mind** when working towards corporate goals.

- **I have improved testing processes to create greater efficiency**. For example, templates I created have been published to the company's quality assurance website for use by other professionals in North America.

I am seeking a new challenge that will tie together my core professional talents with an organization in need of an **expert in testing and technical quality assurance**. My past experience has prepared me for the position you are seeking to fill, and I would welcome the opportunity to meet and further discuss my qualifications.

Sincerely,

Sarah Nguyen

Enclosure: Resume

The bold design of the heading makes an immediate positive impression, and that professional image is reinforced by content that addresses the top skills needed for the position. Bold type accents key terms.

Jennifer Miller, CPRW, CARW, CRS • Professional Edge Resumes • www.ProfessionalEdgeResumes.com

Nigel Watson

Director, IT | Strategic Data Management
resolve issues & meet challenges with exceptional problem solving,
deftly balanced with a focus on bottom line impact

May 15, 2017

Ms. Cynthia Dale, VP of Human Resources
Big Data USA
475 Data Drive
Detroit, MI 48213

RE: DIRECTOR, DATABASE MANAGEMENT

Dear Ms. Dale:

The position of Director, Database Management, at Big Data USA is at the top of my list as an ideal "next challenge" in my 15-year technical career. Echoing your company's focus on innovation, my career has included finding the best path to new technologies and leading groups delivering the complex and the new.

I've often introduced software features that realized SLA benefits, with metrics indicating efficiency, reliability, and robustness. Without fail, my strategies achieve cost savings, often considerable.

My resume demonstrates how I have developed the knowledge and each of the skills that you're looking for. As detailed in your position criteria, I possess:

✓ strong knowledge of database systems, including Oracle and SQL Server;
✓ strong knowledge of data disciplines—database modeling, archiving, quality, and profiling;
✓ strong knowledge of integration platforms; and
✓ strong knowledge of IT security and compliance architectures, programs, and processes.

My goals are always to lead my teams to realize exceptional results and cost savings, ensure quality, and manage risk. I would enjoy meeting with you for further discussion.

Sincerely,

Nigel Watson

Encl: resume

905.555.1111 | nwatson@newleaf.com | LinkedIn.com/NigelWatson–IT

A striking heading, subject line, and footer quickly capture attention. The letter is very readable because of its tightly written paragraphs and bullet points that highlight specific skills and knowledge per the job posting.

Stephanie Clark, BA, MRW, MCRS • New Leaf Resumes • www.newleafresumes.com

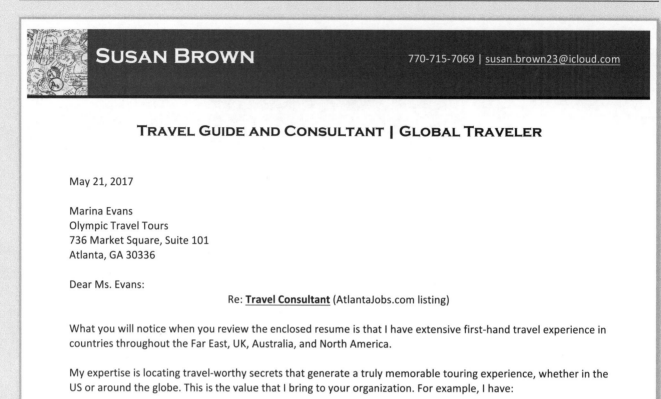

SUSAN BROWN

770-715-7069 | susan.brown23@icloud.com

TRAVEL GUIDE AND CONSULTANT | GLOBAL TRAVELER

May 21, 2017

Marina Evans
Olympic Travel Tours
736 Market Square, Suite 101
Atlanta, GA 30336

Dear Ms. Evans:

Re: **Travel Consultant** (AtlantaJobs.com listing)

What you will notice when you review the enclosed resume is that I have extensive first-hand travel experience in countries throughout the Far East, UK, Australia, and North America.

My expertise is locating travel-worthy secrets that generate a truly memorable touring experience, whether in the US or around the globe. This is the value that I bring to your organization. For example, I have:

- Developed travel itineraries from scratch and made last-minute arrangements dictated by a country's instability—whether climate changes or unrest in the region.

- Experienced the world's cuisine, unforgettable shopping experiences, and unique cultural attractions— giving me the knowledge to tailor travel experiences to each client's interests.

- Gained valuable insight into each country's culture and developed long-term relationships with local travel agencies—thus ensuring that last-minute changes are handled with minimal disruption.

- Completed extensive study and certification in Travel and Tourism from California State University.

I understand what the traveler seeks when making those all-important and often expensive travels plans, and I have no greater satisfaction than providing exceptional itineraries that will create lifetime memories.

I will telephone next week in hopes of scheduling a meeting to discuss how I can assist Olympic Travel Tours in providing outstanding travel services.

Sincerely,

Susan Brown

Enclosure: Resume

A colorful heading and bold headline immediately set the stage for this travel professional. In the letter, she connects both her personal and professional travel experiences to the exact needs of the employer and clients.

Gayle Keefer • TruMark Resume Writing Services • www.trumarkresumes.com

JULIE PETERS

www.linkedin/in/juliepeters ▪ San Francisco, CA ▪ (415) 246-7179 ▪ juliepeters@gmail.com

May 10, 2017

Paul Sutton, CEO
IBeam Technologies
220 Bridge Parkway, Suite #20
Redwood City, CA 94065

RE: SVP, Sales and New Business Development

Dear Mr. Sutton:

As a global business leader, I've had ongoing success driving unprecedented growth in domestic and international medical device and healthcare markets through targeted product diversification, clear priority direction, and strategic partnerships. This comparison outlines some of my achievements as a senior executive relevant to your expectations:

Expectations	My Track Record
Revenue Growth	■ Spurred revenue growth by **17%** during year of economic decline. ■ Propelled sales from zero to more than **$200M in 2 years**.
Profit Growth	■ Cut operating expenses by **$3M** and improved gross margins **190 bps** despite global economic headwind. ■ Improved operating income for the division by **38%**.
Brand Development	■ Transformed brand image and customer experience through reengineered strategic vision. ■ Generated **30%** growth in orders in 1 year.
Market Expansion	■ Exceeded revenue goals by **$100M** over 5 years through strategic acquisitions, partnerships, and geographic expansion. ■ Acquired and integrated **$15M** German entity, meeting and exceeding all stated acquisition financial and strategic targets.

Mr. Sutton, I am confident I can contribute to the achievement of your objectives for growth and success at IBeam. I look forward to a meeting and will call next week.

Sincerely,

Julie Peters

A side-by-side comparison instantly shows how this candidate has performed relevant to very specific expectations in the job posting. The letter is easy to skim and clearly communicates value and success.

Emily Wong, MIM, ACRW, CPRW • Words of Distinction • www.wordsofdistinction.net

ARTHUR JOHNSON

Relocating to Cheyenne, WY • 757-662-9595 • ajexpertsales@mac.com

February 25, 2017

Robin Escobar
Region Mortgage Solutions
258 Overton Lane, Suite 658
Cheyenne, WY 82008

Dear Ms. Escobar:

As a **sales growth expert**, I have contributed to vastly increased revenues at every company I've worked for. It is this expertise that I am offering as your next **Sales & Marketing Director.**

A few highlights of my experience include:

~Sales Growth: I have been a growth driver for the last 4 years, as indicated by these results:

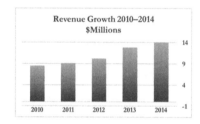

♦ *2016 — $14M*   ♦ *2013 — $9.1M*

♦ *2015 — $12.8M*   ♦ *2012 — $8.5M*

♦ *2014 — $10.2M*

I am persistent in identifying and capturing new opportunities for solid market penetration.

~Customer Relations: Having managed successful relationships with 8K+ loyal customers, I understand how to identify needs, provide solutions, and manage the entire sales cycle.

~Marketing: With extensive experience developing the marketing and outreach materials for tradeshows and corporate events, I am highly skilled in sales and branding techniques. I know what it takes to secure leads and capture new clients.

Ms. Escobar, I am committed to turning customers into loyal advocates for Region Mortgage Solutions.

I am travelling to Cheyenne next week and would welcome the opportunity to meet with you in person to discuss this position in detail. I can be reached at 757-662-9595 to arrange an interview. Thank you.

Sincerely,

Arthur Johnson

The graph showing sales results is the most striking feature of this letter. The reader can clearly see that this candidate has increased sales every year for 5 consecutive years. The remaining content emphasizes additional value in customer relations and marketing—both extremely important.

Sophia Marshall, MHR, ACRW, BCC • Me Sheet • www.mesheet.com

From: **Jacob Helfer,** jacobhelfer@gmail.com
Subject: **Job ID 234106**—Business Development Executive with foresight to anticipate market needs
Date: April 30, 2017
To: **Dave Donato,** dave@donlenco.com

Dear Mr. Donato:

It is unusual to find a business development professional who has the technical know-how to reinvent market strategies and create new revenue streams. Yet that is what I've done time and again throughout my career.

At Blackberry, it was seeing how pivoting the distribution strategy could speed up growth. At Motorola, it was collaborating to design a new product that could penetrate the MSO market.

My strategies have amounted to millions of dollars in revenue for my employers.

I would welcome the opportunity to interview for the position of VP Business Development and discuss how I can create new revenue streams for Donlen.

Jacob Helfer
----
jacobhelfer@gmail.com
630-123-4567
www.linkedin.com/in/jacobhelfer

Attachment: Resume

This is an excellent example of how a tightly written e-note can capture attention, convey valuable information, and get the reader excited to learn more—all in just a few short paragraphs.

Michelle Robin, NCRW, CPRW • Brand Your Career • www.brandyourcareer.com

PETER WATSON, JR.

Boston, MA ▪ 857-330-2753 ▪ peterwatsonjr@gmail.com

February 27, 2017

Ms. Anne Stewart, SVP—Corporate Properties
Davidson Enterprises, Inc.
1422 Broadway Street
Cambridge, MA 02138

Subject: General Manager, SleepWell Properties

Dear Ms. Stewart:

The hotel/hospitality industry is well known for multiple business challenges—high staff turnover, variable occupancy rates, and diverse competitive pressures. Despite those challenges, I have established a record in the industry for not only meeting but exceeding revenue and profit goals.

After reviewing your requirements for a General Manager and researching Davidson's business situation, I believe you will find value in the following examples of my management contributions:

- **Hyatt Place-Concord:** Increased revenue 30% during the first year.

- **Courtyard by Marriott–Brighton:** Increased revenue more than 8% within four months during major renovation activity.

- **Courtyard by Marriott–Framingham:** Achieved a premium RevPar index within four months despite widespread travel impact from the September 2001 attack.

- **Boston Regency Place Hotel:** Maintained strong guest satisfaction, including zero noise complaints, during Boston's massive "Big Dig" construction project close to the hotel's entrance.

Based on my record of results, I believe it would be mutually beneficial for us to meet to discuss the specific challenges and opportunities your organization is facing. As your General Manager, I can ensure that we meet the challenges and take full advantage of the opportunities.

I will telephone on Friday to schedule an interview.

Sincerely,

Peter Watson, Jr.

Enclosure: Resume

The theme of "challenges and opportunities" specific to the hospitality industry is introduced in the first paragraph and carried through the entire letter. Four strong bullet points provide specific examples that will be of great interest to the reader and clearly demonstrate that this job seeker delivers results.

Georgia Adamson, MRW, ACRW, CPRW, CJSS, CEIP • A Successful Career • www.ablueribbonresume.com

From: **Rosemarie Taylor,** rjtaylor@yahoo.com

Subject: **Manufacturing Manager**—P&G & Bacardi Experience, US & International

Date: April 30, 2017

To: Job34567@theladders.com

During more than 10 years in leadership positions with Procter & Gamble and Bacardi Bottling Corp. in North America, Europe, and Asia, I have delivered cost savings, production efficiencies, innovative packaging initiatives, and successful product launches.

A few highlights from my current role as Director of Product Manufacturing for Bacardi:

- **Cut 20% of cost from our #1 production line** by reducing cost of goods and increasing efficiency.
- **Slashed number of SKUs 50%,** driving measurable gains in quality while reducing product cost.
- **Exceeded first-year sales goal by 37%** and led the most successful product launch in company history.

I'm confident I can continue my track record of contributions as your Manufacturing Manager and would appreciate the opportunity to learn more about this opportunity.

Sincerely,

Rosemarie Taylor

904-555-1357—Call or text

rjtaylor@yahoo.com

http://www.linkedin.com/in/rosemarietaylor

Resume attached as PDF

This e-note gets right to the point, sharing general and then specific (and highly relevant) achievements from 10 years of experience in similar roles. No follow-up is promised—nor is it possible, because this is a "blind" posting so there is no individual with whom to follow up.

Louise Kursmark, MRW, CPRW, CCM, JCTC, CEIP • Best Impression Career Services • www.louisekursmark.com

Ellie Whitney

Riverside, CA 92508 ▪ 951-242-9799 ▪ ellie.whitney@yahoo.com ▪ LinkedIn

Director of Finance | Corporate Controller

Healthcare Tax Accounting ▪ Strategic/Financial Planning ▪ HR Administration ▪ Business Management

January 15, 2017

John Peterson
United Capital Healthcare
3709 United Rd
Newport Beach, CA 92658

Dear Mr. Peterson:

Re: Director of Finance—LinkedIn Job Posting

As a senior accounting and finance executive, my priority is to ensure the most accurate financial information while leading efforts to constantly improve operations and maximize efficiency.

For instance, during my most recent role at Agape Medical Management, I led a 45-person team and controlled a $15M budget. I was honored to be selected to direct efforts of centralizing the accounts payable department after our merger with Pierce Healthcare Systems.

Under my direction, we were able to make a seamless transition that produced substantial wins:

- Saved more than $2.5M in operational costs.
- Cut AP processing time from 7 days to 3 days.
- Successfully integrated new systems with no negative impact to our clients.

This tremendous success stemmed from not only my analytical thought process, but the capability to motivate employees to produce the accurate reporting practices necessary to ensure sound financial operations.

Your current opening for a Director of Finance is exciting and seems an excellent fit for my financial expertise. Feel free to contact me at your earliest convenience to further discuss how I can contribute to United Capital Healthcare's continued financial stability and longevity.

Sincerely,

Ellie P. Whitney

Notice how easy it is to quickly skim this letter. The paragraphs are short, but each is packed with information of value and relevance to this particular position with this specific employer. The heading, carried over from the resume, highlights keywords, relevant areas of experience, and valuable traits.

Melanie Denny, MBA • Resume-Evolution • www.resume-evolution.com

CHARLES P. BAKER, JD, CDP

(616) 902-4686 | cpbaker@gmail.com | linkedin.com/in/charlespbaker

SENIOR DIVERSITY EXECUTIVE

January 3, 2017

Mr. Dennis Bardos
Vice President, Global Inclusion
State Street Inc.
One Lincoln Street
Boston, MA 02111

Dear Mr. Bardos:

I am writing to express my interest in the recent posting for the **Chief Diversity Officer** (CDO) position with State Street and have attached my resume for your review.

My 10+ years of strategy, diversity, and inclusion experience across multiple industries—real estate, healthcare, technology, public service, and manufacturing—demonstrates a unique combination of talent and drive.

Relevant to your stated needs, my experience includes:

- **Strategic Planning & Leadership**—Repeatedly recruited to establish the strategic direction and long-term organizational approach to diversity and inclusion, I have filled this role at BankCorp, Hill & Dale, and Acme.

- **New Program Implementation**—I am known for instilling best practices in all layers of the organization, then developing performance-monitoring protocols and reporting tools to ensure sustainability.

- **Community & Employee Engagement**—At each company we achieved significant gains in recruitment and retention of diverse talent, as well as employee participation in community outreach initiatives.

As a highly accomplished diversity professional, I bring a focused application of process innovation, technology, and continuous improvement to ensure alignment of best practices on a global scale. My extensive investment in continuing education demonstrates not only a commitment to—but a passion for—diversity and inclusion.

I welcome the opportunity for a personal interview and will follow up next week to schedule a time that is convenient. Thank you.

Sincerely,

Charles P. Baker

Enclosure

> Using bullets to highlight specific areas of experience and accomplishment makes these important qualifications stand out. Toward the end of the letter this job seeker also communicates his passion for his work, adding a personal element to the hard skills and qualifications previously shared.

Kris McGuigan, ACRW, CCMC • Professional Courage LLC • professionalcourage.com

From:	**Erik Jensen,** erikjensen@gmail.com
Subject:	**EVP, Global Product Development**
Date:	February 19, 2017
To:	**Abby Hockett,** abby.hockett@sanjanetworks.com

Dear Ms. Hockett:

As SVP of Development at Astra Networks, I led my team to achieve first prize at the *Silicon Valley Internet-of-Things Challenge Competition 2016*—one of the most prestigious awards for driving innovation. Now, I'd like to bring my **20 years of experience steering successful IoT product initiatives** to Sanja Networks.

Prior to working for Astra, I was a company founder and SVP of Product Development at Yanzi, a leading B2B provider of portable interactive technology. We sold Yanzi in 2014 after reaching $34M in sales and twice earning recognition from Deloitte as one of the fastest growing startups in Silicon Valley.

I was also a senior consultant for a product realization consortium, where I conducted architecture and design reviews to create roadmaps for startups in the development of embedded control systems for smart home and automotive (V2X) products.

A tireless tinkerer, I'm the inventor of more than 30 US and international patents, and I'm committed to infusing the same excitement for innovation into the teams I lead.

As a startup in the competitive field of IoT, Sanja Networks demands a leader who complements an engineering background with the ability to guide your organization toward a focused vision for groundbreaking technology.

I'm that leader, and I look forward to speaking with you in the near future about the EVP Global Product Development position at Sanja Networks.

Sincerely,

Erik Jensen
=========================
415-288-2951
erikjensen@gmail.com
www.linkedin.com/in/ejensen

Resume attached

Starting with a notable award, this letter is chock-full of experiences and achievements that will be of significant interest to the reader. The job seeker makes a very strong case that he is true veteran and leader in the emerging arena of the Internet of Things (IoT).

Emily Wong, MIM, ACRW, CPRW • Words of Distinction • www.wordsofdistinction.net

From:	**Nancy Mellers,** nancymellers@wahoo.com
Subject:	**VP Information Systems/CTO**
Date:	June 3, 2017
To:	**Seth Bailey,** baileyseth@pittresearch.com

Dear Mr. Bailey:

With 15 years of experience managing IT projects and teams for a Fortune 100 company, I am well prepared to serve as your Chief Technology Officer.

Just a few examples of the value I offer Pitt Research and Development:

- **Global Project Planning and Leadership:** At Silica Networks I direct a diverse team conducting information assurance projects and vulnerability management across 3 enterprise networks encompassing 1,200 devices and 400 users worldwide.

- **Data Reliability and Security:** We have amassed an outstanding record by any metrics imaginable. I would be pleased to share details with you when we meet.

- **IT Operations:** With employees and customers spanning the globe, I have led projects and managed operations in 30 different countries on 4 continents. I am at my best managing complex and diverse technologies, operations, and teams.

- **C-Level Consulting:** Currently, I deliver multiple weekly briefings to 26 senior business leaders.

In addition to the accomplishments highlighted in my attached resume, I offer you a passion for seeing team members reach their full potential and expand their corporate contributions.

I welcome the opportunity to interview for the VP position and look forward to hearing from you.

Sincerely,

Nancy Mellers, MSM, PMP, CISSP

205-555-1212
nancymellers@wahoo.com

This job seeker's strongest qualification is the 15 years she has spent with a major global technology corporation. Her letter "mines" this experience to pull out the most relevant and impressive details and accomplishments to competitively position herself for the advertised opportunity.

Alexia Scott, CPRW • A Winning Resume • http://www.a-winning-resume.com

Paul Merrick, MBA

New York, NY 10024 | (650) 234-5660 | PaulMerrick@gmail.com

BRAND STRATEGY | BUSINESS DEVELOPMENT | CONSUMER MARKETING

April 12, 2017

Ms. Melissa Panetta, Recruiter
American Express Company
200 Vesey Street, 50th Floor
New York, NY 10285

Re: Job ID #16004212, **Senior Manager, Global Strategy & Capabilities (GS&C)—Americas**

Dear Ms. Panetta:

Why am I the right candidate? Because I can readily address the 3 priorities of this important role:

- *Know and Win the Customer*—As the *"Account Executive to Watch"* at NBC, I secured more than $9M annually in sponsorship deals by researching the market, building relationships, and understanding all of my clients' unique needs and pain points.

- *Improve the Core*—At Capital Two, I designed 7 innovative and interactive web/multimedia programs that advanced strategic corporate goals for customer acquisition, customer retention, social media influence, and innovation. The success of these programs allowed us eliminate all print and direct-mail advertising, saving $400K annually.

- *Accelerate Merchant Acquisition & Enable Client Self-Management*—When Capital Two introduced tap-and-pay systems, I led the rollout of information programs that helped boost merchant acquisition 12% above goal and led 92% of customers to use the new system.

I am confident that I have the capability, determination, and resources to fully support *and propel* the GS&C team in launching new programs, expanding into new markets, and supporting strategic business goals.

I would appreciate the opportunity to further discuss my qualifications and potential contributions in delivering the best-in-class, premium merchant customer experience that is expected of the Amex brand. I look forward to meeting with you and will follow up in just a few days.

Sincerely,

Paul Merrick

This letter provides specific examples of experience and success in the 3 areas that were listed as the top priorities for this position. The job seeker further customizes the letter with a reference to the company and its brand in the closing paragraph, demonstrating extra effort and interest.

Kate Madden, MBA, CPRW • Fresh Start Resumes, LLC • www.freshstartresumes.com

CHAPTER 3:
Cold Call Letters

What Is a Cold Call Letter?

A cold call letter is unsolicited. Rather than responding to a specific job posting, you're contacting a company or recruiter to explore opportunities that might exist now or in the future. Consider these 2 scenarios when you might write a cold call letter:

- If you have an interest in working for a specific company, yet the company has no active job postings that are relevant, send a cold call letter to express your interest. You never know what's happening inside an organization and when they might have a need for someone with your skills and experience. Nothing ventured … nothing gained.

- Use cold call letters to introduce yourself to recruiters who specialize in your industry and/or profession. Recruiters are often looking for top-quality candidates for both current and future engagements.

As you learned in previous chapters, you can write an e-note or a more formal cover letter. Either is acceptable for a cold call letter and, in fact, for all letters that we'll share throughout this book.

> **Pro Tip: A cold call letter faces 2 distinct challenges.** Just like a job posting letter, a cold call letter will present your qualifications. More importantly, to ensure that it will be read, it must instantly engage your audience because, at least publicly, they are not advertising for a candidate with your skill set.

It is important to note that cold call letters are not the most effective way to generate interest during your job search. Of course, they can and do work! But if you are targeting a particular company, it is much more effective to approach the company through a networking contact or referral. You'll read all about those 2 types of letters in Chapters 5 and 6.

What Do You Want to Achieve in Your Cold Call Letter?

Your #1 goal in writing a cold call letter is to make an instant connection with the employer or recruiter so they will want to know more and grant you the opportunity for an interview.

Here are the most frequent scenarios for sending this type of letter:

- **It's a company that you have always wanted to work for** because of what it does, the industry and markets it serves, the products and services it delivers, its reputation within its industry, its civic and philanthropic efforts, or a host of other reasons.

- **It's a company that has many job postings,** even though they're not the right positions for you. The high level of activity might indicate that the company is ramping up, expanding, and/or otherwise in need of additional talent. By sending a cold call letter in advance of a possible hiring need, you can potentially put yourself in a leading position for a job that might be on the horizon.

- **It's a recruiting firm that specializes in your industry or profession.** Even if they are not currently advertising a position for you, they are likely to be on the lookout for good candidates for future searches. You can put yourself on their radar screen (in their database) ahead of the competition.

- **In your research to find a new job, you have read a lot about a particular company.** Perhaps it's completing an acquisition, building a new facility, launching a new product line, or otherwise engaged in noteworthy activities. Be proactive! Send a letter that tells the people in a position to hire you why the company has caught your interest and why you're a qualified candidate for positions they may need to fill.

How Do You Write a Cold Call Letter?

Remember, your first goal is to instantly capture attention. Give the recipient a reason to read your letter even though, as far as you know, they're not actively hiring—at least not for a job that's suitable for you.

Begin your letter by explaining why you're writing to them. As noted in the previous section, you might reference their newest acquisition and how you would fit into the evolving organization, comment on a new product line that's similar to products you've designed or sold in the past, recognize the achievements of a particular individual within the company, or commend them on a new product launch.

If writing to a recruiter, you might acknowledge that the firm is well known in its particular niche or reference all of the job postings you've seen from them. *Note: Be sure to review Chapter 4 for additional recruiter-specific advice, insights, and samples.*

> **Pro Tip: Make an instant connection between yourself and the company or recruiting firm when writing a cold call letter.** A decision maker won't be interested if your letter appears to be a mass-mail message—that's impersonal and off-putting. Tell them specifically why you chose to contact them so that they know you are a thoughtful and well-informed job seeker.

What type of information might you share that would be of interest to a hiring manager, human resources professional, recruiter, or other decision maker? Here are a few ideas:

- Your deep and rich experience in their industry.

- Expertise in a specific product, technology, service, or operation.

- Something about yourself that is unique, memorable, distinctive, or rare and that could be of great value to them—such as customer contacts, international experience, language skills, influential connections, hard-to-find technology skills, or other relevant information.

- Specific and quantifiable achievements that quickly represent the positive impact you've had on your previous employers.

- Strong work history and professional experience that is relevant to the company that you're targeting.

- Upper-tier educational and/or professional credentials.

- Personal information that somehow connects you to the company, its industry, and/or its products and services. Although unusual, this approach has proven to be extremely effective when the personal information instantly resonates with the reader.

Pro Tip: You can never write a generic cold call letter. Each letter *must* be written to address the individual needs of that particular company—today's needs or those in the future.

To enhance the potential for a positive response after you've submitted your cold call letter, you must follow up. Remember, the company decision maker or recruiter did not post a specific job, they're not focused on new hires, and they didn't ask for your letter. Don't just wish and hope for them to get in touch with you. In your letter, request a personal interview and promise to follow up … and then do so!

How Do You Submit a Cold Call Letter?

We recommend that you email your letter. To capture the reader's attention as quickly as possible, use the e-note format and paste your content into the body of the email message. Then, attach your resume as a PDF (our recommendation) or Word document.

You might consider snail mail as another alternative for submitting your cold call letter. People are overwhelmed with email and it's easy to hit the delete button. When you send snail mail—a physical letter that lands on someone's desk—your message has a much greater chance of being opened and read.

Who Is the Audience?

The audience for cold call letters can be any company or recruiting firm in any industry in any part of the world. What's most critical is that the specific person or audience that you're targeting has the potential to be interested in you—your qualifications, work experience, achievements, educational and professional credentials, technology skills, and value to the organization.

Your greatest challenge is to capture interest, make your readers eager to know more, and entice them to reach out to you—or to be receptive when you follow up.

To Whom Do You Send It?

Send a cold call letter to introduce yourself to a hiring manager, HR professional, executive, or someone else within a company. For best results, this individual should have the authority to schedule an interview with you or, at the very least, put you in touch with the person who can.

You can also send cold call letters to recruiting and executive search firms that specialize in your industry or profession. For the greatest impact and return on your time, we strongly urge that you *stay in your lane,* as recruiters who specialize in engineering are not interested in a candidate with retail sales experience. Don't waste their time or your effort!

Cold call letters are just that—"cold"—because you are writing to someone you do not know. This is what differentiates them from networking letters—"warm" letters sent to people you do know. We'll write in much greater detail about networking letters in Chapter 5.

> **Pro Tip: The sole reason you're sending a cold call letter is to have a conversation and get an interview.** You don't want a conversation with "anyone"; you want it with a specific person who can help you advance your career. To make the most of your cold call outreach, make the effort to find that person and write a letter that appeals quite specifically to her interests.

For a cold call letter to be effective, it must be written to a person and not just a job title (e.g., Human Resources Director, VP of Marketing, President). If you are really serious about a company, you will have done your research to learn all that you can about the organization, its products and/or services, its people, its culture, and most importantly, where someone with your skills and experience will best fit in.

As part of that research, it's imperative that you find the name of the person whom you want to contact. By writing to someone, as opposed to just anyone, you're demonstrating that you know enough about the company to know who is the right contact. This act, in and of itself, communicates a strong message of your interest in and commitment to a potential new employer.

The best places to find people's names—and often their direct contact information—is on a company's website, its LinkedIn or Facebook page, an individual's LinkedIn profile, or another online directory.

What Are the Unique Characteristics of a Cold Call Letter?

The cold call letters on the following pages—30 professionally written letters created for real job seekers—demonstrate all of the guidelines and principles we've shared in this chapter.

The 30 letters are divided into 3 groups:

- 10 Cold Call Letters for College Graduates, Young Professionals, and Entry-Level Workers (pages 63–72)

- 10 Cold Call Letters for Mid-Career Professionals (pages 73–82)

- 10 Cold Call Letters for Experienced Professionals, Managers, and Executives (pages 83–92)

At the bottom of each letter is a box containing notes and insights that will help you understand the context for each letter and why it was written in the way that it was.

1234 West Rock Creek
Missoula, MT 59801

JENNIFER SMITH

(406) 456-7878
jennsmith@gmail.com

June 1, 2017

Ms. Krystal Kelley, Owner
Desert Models and Talent Agency
South 1951 Palm Canyon Drive
Palm Springs, CA 92263

Dear Ms. Kelley:

A new graduate with a public relations and marketing degree, I spent last year interning for Rocky Mountain Entertainment and Talent Agency representing adults and children for fashion, print, runway talent, voiceovers, and on-camera television and film.

Our clients hold impressive dossiers, including walking elite regional, national, and international fashion shows, appearing in Oscar-winning films, and adding voiceovers for Disney Channel documentary television. I would be thrilled to continue helping talent reach higher success levels through education, training, exposure, and partnering with top modeling agencies, scouts, casting directors, and photographers.

KEY QUALIFICATIONS

TALENT AGENT TRAINEE – MARKETING EVENT COORDINATOR

An ambitious intern, I came to be relied upon for personalized service, strong interpersonal skills, a professional demeanor, and "can-do" attitude.

For glitzy events, I created itineraries and calendars; for castings, I designed Excel spreadsheets; within the industry, I built a reputation for meticulous work. Organized, detailed, and technically savvy, I was praised for successfully coordinating a heavy call volume, confidential client meetings, and high-profile talent bookings.

If you need someone with an eye for talent, strong gut instincts, desk experience, and knowledge of talent representation, we should talk. I look forward to hearing from you. Thank you for your time.

Sincerely,

JENNIFER SMITH
Enclosure: resume

This letter has an eye-catching design—both the photo at the top (perfectly appropriate for an aspiring talent agent) and the centered headline of Key Qualifications. The job seeker's internship is the central story of the narrative that flows smoothly and includes truly pertinent details and experiences.

Cheryl Minnick, Ed.D., NCRW • University of Montana • CMinnick@mso.umt.edu

From: **Landon Johnson,** landonj@gmail.com
Subject: **Referred by John Campbell**
Date: June 7, 2017
To: **Brad Hall,** bhall@nplconstruction

Dear Mr. Hall:

My neighbor, John Campbell (a yard manager at your Bozeman operation), encouraged me to reach out to you. John said that NPL recently signed a contract for a major construction project in Drummond, Montana, and that you might be in need of a Heavy Equipment Operator—exactly the opportunity I am seeking.

From working around farm machinery and construction equipment all my life, I have developed the technical skills, including hand signals and 2-way radio operation, needed to be a heavy equipment operator.

I grew up playing on backhoes at my grandfather's excavating shop and on tractors at our family cattle ranch. Working with my grandfather and father on large and small jobs taught me the value of a Montana work ethic and giving a hard day's work for a day's pay.

Last week, I graduated from high school and am looking for a full-time construction job. If you have an opening for a person with a lifetime of experience operating all types of heavy equipment, machinery, and power tools, I would appreciate an interview. I am excited about the possibility of a career with NPL Construction, and I thank you for your consideration.

Sincerely,

Landon Johnson
406-987-6543 (Call or Text)
landonj@gmail.com

Although no position has been advertised, this job seeker has an inside tip from a current employee, and he opens his letter with that reference. He goes on to tell the story of his upbringing and the experiences that have qualified him for his current career goal.

Cheryl Minnick, Ed.D., NCRW • University of Montana • CMinnick@mso.umt.edu

From: **Charlie Rogers,** charlie.rogers@yahoo.com
Subject: **Jack Bradford suggested I contact you**
Date: May 26, 2017
To: **Cal Jefferies,** ctjefferies@kbhomes.com

Dear Mr. Jefferies:

My friend Jack Bradford has been working for KB Homes for the past year, and he is so enthusiastic about his job and the company that he suggested I contact you to see if there might be a place for me.

A recent graduate of the University of Georgia, I have worked in the construction industry throughout high school and college. I've learned to read construction plans, operate basic tools and machinery, and been promoted based on excelling in the roles I was given.

In addition to new home construction and renovation, over the past 5 years I have worked on a number of large-scale commercial projects, including the Atlanta Botanical, Yerkes Primate Center at Emory University, Hotel Indigo Vinings, and other equally interesting structures.

In addition to my skills and experience, I bring other qualities for which I have been recognized:

➢ Strong <u>interpersonal abilities</u> acquired while working with diverse groups as both a laborer and a supervisor and across all levels of an organization.

➢ Outstanding <u>leadership and teamwork skills</u>, demonstrated by consistently bringing projects in on time and on or under budget.

➢ <u>Broad knowledge of construction methods and practices</u>, developed while working on a wide range of projects over a number of years and in various positions throughout the industry.

I am confident I have developed a professional resourcefulness that will make me a significant asset to KB Homes, and I would welcome the opportunity to speak with you to discuss your needs. You may reach me by phone or email at any time. I look forward to our discussion!

Sincerely,

Charlie Rogers
charlie.rogers@yahoo.com
404-555-1212

P.S. I am willing and able to relocate most anywhere in the US for the right opportunity.

A positive and enthusiastic referral is a great way to begin a general inquiry letter. Good employees are the best source of good new hires for many companies, so hiring managers take such referrals very seriously. This letter details skills and experiences that would be relevant to many potential positions in the construction industry.

From: **David Hattersley,** dhattersley@hattersleymail.com
Subject: **International Business Leadership Program at Global Financial**
Date: June 2, 2017
To: **Martha Motley,** mmotley@globalfinancial.com

Dear Ms. Motley:

I was intrigued by the International Business Leadership Program I read about in the Cincinnati Business Courier. The rotational opportunities described in the article really piqued my interest. After further research, I concluded that your company's goals are a good fit for my analytical and creative skills and interest in international finance. Coupled with this, I bring energy, enthusiasm, and eagerness to learn and contribute.

As a graduating International Business and Finance major at Xavier University, I am confident I bring up-to-date knowledge and skills that will prove beneficial to your efforts in Treasury Services. My overseas internship at European Enterprises provided invaluable insight into some of the financing challenges associated with opening a new R&D facility—an area I know your company is actively pursuing.

I assisted the CFO of European Enterprises with evaluating different financing options and got the opportunity to sit in on meetings with foreign banks. I was able to learn first-hand how different proposals are evaluated and was really excited when the CFO asked me to develop a comparative analysis of the options. I used my Excel skills to good effect as I offered my recommendation, which coincided exactly with how the company settled!

I would welcome the opportunity to discuss some of my other experiences in more detail and have attached my resume for your review.

Thank you for your consideration, and I look forward to meeting you in the near future.

Sincerely,

David Hattersley
Cincinnati, OH | dhattersley@hattersleymail.com | 513-727-4567

This job seeker shows his knowledge of the company by referencing a specific program that he read about in the local press and then went on to research. His effort communicates a lot of positive attributes of this candidate. He goes on to tell a brief, relevant story that showcases his skills and his potential.

Barry Joffe • Career Development Partners • barryjoffe@cinci.rr.com

Samuel Leghorn Jannsen

Northern Shores, New York · 202-123-9876 · sam.leghorn.jannsen@gmail.com

Retail Sales & Marketing Whiz

January 19, 2017

Drake's General Stores
ATTN: Ms. Faree T. Bell
12345 6th Street
New York, NY 11122

Re: Retail Manager

Dear Ms. Bell:

Could you use a little magic to boost your retail sales, your staff retention, and your bottom line? I offer you no sleight-of-hand, just solid numbers and satisfied customers!

For the past 3 years I helped manage retail locations for Houdini's Magic, and it is no illusion: We set new sales records, re-ignited profits, and raised customer satisfaction levels—almost like magic! With the proper training, the right product selection, professional attitudes, and perseverance, our stores have gained a reputation for product quality and employee satisfaction. We:

- Increased sales last year by 42% in a recessionary market.
- Doubled profitability this past year, due in part to implementing JIT inventory and reducing overhead.
- Levitated employee retention via improved training/mentoring and cost-effective incentives.
- Followed up sales with digital surveys and discovered that we have charmed our customers.

When you're ready to conjure up stronger profits, call me. I would love to make them appear for you, too.

Very truly yours,

Samuel Leghorn Jannsen

Resume attached

With a "magical" theme running throughout, this letter is clever and fun to read. But it's much more than that: It includes strong, specific, and relevant achievements, and it makes a great case that this candidate would be a real asset to any retail management team.

Debra O'Reilly, CPRW, CEIP, JCTC, CG3C, CJSS • A First Impression Resume Service • http://resumewriter.com

From: **Cliff Walker,** cliffordwalker2@gmail.com

Subject: **Strategic Sales Specialist—Won $5M Enterprise Contract, 185% of Sales Target**

Date: May 30, 2017

To: **James Bailey,** james.bailey@hitech.com

Mr. Bailey:

Are you looking for a high-tech sales specialist who can fast-track peak sales performance and profitability?

With a deep perspective on how fit-for-purpose technology solutions drive business growth and a proven record of selling complex concepts that clients didn't know they needed, I've attached my resume detailing how I:

- ✓ **Propelled sales 300% in 2 years** as Xerox's top revenue producer in the region after winning a **$5M first-of-its-kind deal with the Illinois State Senate** and a similar **$4M agreement with GB Power Systems.**

- ✓ **Orchestrated $7M in future sales** for a new energy division at Kumin Industrial Technologies and vitalized a formerly neglected market, **developing a thriving territory that spanned 7 states and Canada.**

- ✓ Positioned Wolmac Company to **edge out its #1 competitor** and **built a $6.5M sales pipeline** by winning meetings and accounts with presumably "unreachable" power players at 3 of the 10 largest global banks.

I would appreciate a confidential chat to explore opportunities and discuss how I can duplicate comparable successes for HiTech. I'll follow up with you this week to schedule an initial discussion. Thank you.

Cliff Walker

****

Cell: **923.455.9941**
Email: cliffordwalker2@gmail.com

Attachment: Resume

The subject line of this e-note includes compelling evidence of value, and the letter provides more specifics about the job seeker's relevant sales achievements. The entire letter is very crisp, with all paragraphs just 2 lines long after an opening question that is formatted (bold, italic, centered, and in color) to capture attention.

Sandra Ingemansen, CERM, CMRW, CPRW, CJSS • Resume Strategies • http://www.resume-strategies.com

Kevin Roberts

719-453-6292 | kevinrobertsevents@gmail.com | www.linkedin.com/in/KevinRobertsEvents

February 1, 2017

Joan Smith
JS Events
507 Maple Street
Denver, CO 80911

Dear Ms. Smith:

Are you considering expanding your event management staff? If so, my experience will be of interest to you!

I produce events and multimedia presentations that engage people through creative and memorable experiences. In 3 years with the region's largest locally owned media company, I supported and planned projects reaching more than 10,000 subscribers and 20,000 social media followers.

For example, I …

- Coordinated an annual music festival with 800 attendees and 25 performers on average.
- Created marketing communications and social media content for a "Best Of" special publication, a major philanthropy campaign, and an online marketplace highlighting local businesses.
- Developed consistent messaging for themed events tied to each company's or sponsor's strategic brand.

Equally important is my ability to tackle challenges with composure. For example, when faced with significant parking challenges for the annual music festival, I brokered deals with lot owners and coordinated a shuttle service so that attendees could focus on the performances without driving in circles.

I would appreciate the opportunity to talk about how I can create and deliver memorable events for JS Event's clients. I have included my resume and will call on Wednesday to follow up.

Sincerely,

Kevin Roberts

Why are you writing? This letter answers that important question immediately, then goes on to highlight specific experiences and capabilities that should interest the reader. Notice the precise follow-up mentioned in the closing paragraph. This job seeker is taking control of his search with a proactive approach to getting the interview.

Dodie Thompson, CPRW, CEIP • Peak Resumes, LLC • www.peakresumes.com

DANIEL MAITLAND, BSc Geology

"The principle is...about being better than you were the day before."
~Steve Young

216-88 Albert Lake Rd ▪ Calgary, AB P6A 5C1
P: 705.421.2131 ▪ E: dmaitland@gmail.com ▪ LI: ca.linkedin.com/in/danielmaitland

March 4, 2017

Mr. Rob Smith
Esso Petroleum Centre
25 Lake Street
Fort McMurray, AB P2B 1X1

RE: Operations Geologist

Dear Mr. Smith:

A solutions-focused and internally motivated Wellsite Geologist with 5 years' experienced, I produced impressive results for my clients, and I am now seeking a new opportunity. Having been a part of operations across Alberta, I bring extensive experience and knowledge related to well development, including identifying potential locations to drill and assisting the drill team.

What sets me apart? I collaboratively work with team members to understand limitations in data, combine this with other real-time MWD data and drill cuttings, and compare and assign weight and value to this data to make critical decisions.

Here's an example: When a directional driller gives me a survey point, I don't just take this as fact. I roughly calculate an ellipse of error and use my offset well data to learn exactly where we are, relative to the formation, and where we need to be. I then use the real-time survey data to make decisions and work in partnership with the directional driller.

As your next operations geologist, I will bring this critical thinking and leadership style with me.

What's next? Although my resume outlines my experience, a personal meeting would allow us to have a two-way conversation. It would be a pleasure to meet with you to share insights into our ever-changing industry and learn more about how I can help Esso Petroleum attain its objectives.

Sincerely,

Daniel Maitland, BSc Geology

The bold introductions to each paragraph make this letter easy to skim and create a logical flow from beginning to end to tell a great story. It's interesting, engaging, and proactive regarding next steps. Also notable is the attractive heading and attention-getting quote that offers a glimpse into the job seeker's character.

Skye Berry-Burke, CMRW, CRS, CIS, CES • Sky is The Limit • www.skyeisthelimit.ca

From:	**Yogesh Krishnara,** yogeshkrishnara@gmail.com
Subject:	**Environmental Testing Opportunities**
Date:	June 4, 2017
To:	**Mark Nicholas,** mnicholas@aquapuresystems.com

Dear Mr. Nicholas:

My expertise in comprehensive environmental testing can help you enhance your productivity and reduce costs.

I have 7 years of experience in the operation and maintenance of:

- auto samplers
- sample concentrators
- gas chromatographs
- mass spectrometers

My ability to complete sample collection and lab procedures with speed and accuracy has reduced customer complaints considerably, allowing for increased business.

Due to my solid work ethic and superior knowledge of chemistry and instrumentation, my employers often selected me for beta testing when new methods were introduced. They knew I was always open to new challenges and could be counted on to get the job done, even if it meant coming in early, staying late, or working weekends.

A large part of my work involved ordering parts and supplies, which I handled in a very organized and efficient manner so that we could respond to urgent requests at a moment's notice. I ensured all equipment was functioning properly, often thinking and acting quickly to fix many problems myself to avoid costly delays.

As a member of your laboratory team, I am certain I would be a valued asset toward achieving your goals. If you have an opening that would fit my capabilities, I would be very glad to meet with you for further discussion.

Sincerely,

Yogesh Krishnara
~~~~~~~~~~~~~~~~~~
[213] 868-2837 — call or text
yogeshkrishnara@gmail.com
42-03 Pacific Parkway, Apartment 9, Los Angeles, CA 90052

This e-note opens with a bold statement of the job seeker's capabilities and potential impact. Although job details are unknown because there is no posted opening, the letter presents both broad qualifications and specific contributions relevant to the role of environmental tester.

Melanie Noonan • Peripheral Pro LLC • PeriPro1@aol.com

RUSSELL GELLER

russellgeller20@gmail.com • 847-123-9876
www.linkedin.com/in/russellgeller

May 21, 2017

Ms. Nancy Zukowski
Director of Marketing
Harley-Davidson Motor Company
3700 W. Juneau Avenue
Milwaukee, WI 53208

Dear Ms. Zukowski:

My expertise is creating visibility, building engagement, and generating business through social media.

When I respond to negative comments on social media, it's like using my keyboard to defuse a bomb. I artfully craft my response to help turn a detractor into a promoter. This is just one way I have been successful managing social media, and I would now like to bring those skills to Harley-Davidson in the role of Social Media Manager.

In my career, I have started new processes in web content, public relations, and social media for motor industry organizations. Highlights include:

- ➤ Initiated sending samples with press releases so media could test and review gear.
- ➤ Conducted first-ever live press event for ICON Motosports.
- ➤ Took initiative to introduce a motorcycle subsection for Bullz-eye.com.

I am confident I can help Harley-Davidson grow your social media presence and customer base. I would like the opportunity to meet with you to discuss your needs and ways I can help.

Sincerely,

Russell Geller

Resume attached

First clearly establishing what he does well, this job seeker then goes on to share his approach to managing social media in ways that benefit his employers. The 3 bulleted items that follow illustrate his skills in action and are totally on-point for the industry he's targeting.

Michelle Robin, NCRW, CPRW • Brand Your Career • http://www.brandyourcareer.com

Bohdan Zorian

Email: bzorian@newleaf.com
Skype: boh.zor
Cell: 252 69 96952

Automotive Mechanic / Equipment Service Technician
~ top-notch technical ability, commitment to organizational goals, and a real team player ~

May 20, 2017

Mr. A. Halliwell
Northern Pipeline, Inc.

Re: Heavy Equipment Technician

Dear Mr. Halliwell:

If you're looking for a mechanic who has exceptional technical skills and **can fix "anything,"** works well in a team environment, and is recognized as highly productive, then your search may be over.

Up to now, my 20+ years as a Mechanic have been spent in Europe and most recently in the Middle East, where I added armored vehicles, airport equipment, and other heavy equipment to my set of engine repair skills.

Since 2007, my job has taken me to dangerous or environmentally challenging environments, working for multinational providers of mining, drilling, and construction services. **My technical skills came in handy at times when inventory was unavailable and innovative problem solving was needed**. My current manager remarked that he has not seen one vehicle that I could not fix.

I have repaired many vehicle models of which I had no prior knowledge and certainly no specialized technical training. I guarantee that I would soon become the go-to expert for Northern Pipeline's vehicles.

In addition, I learned to use MS Word and Excel as well as databases related to placing orders and monitoring inventory levels.

Finally, I wish to share that I have a positive attitude, I really enjoy my work, and I like sharing my knowledge with junior staff.

If my skills, knowledge, and attitude sound perfect for your business, please email. I am available to arrange a Skype interview or phone call at your convenience. Thank you.

Bohdan Zorian

Encl: resume

** P.S. I scored top marks for quality of work, quantity of work, flexibility, dependability, and attendance in last year's performance evaluation.

Mentioning both technical skills and personal attributes, this letter paints the picture of a highly valuable employee. Bold type is used throughout to call attention to key points. Notice the P.S.—an attention-getting and powerful footnote to an already strong letter.

Stephanie Clark, BA, MRW, MCRS • New Leaf Resumes • www.newleafresumes.com

From: **Robert Scott,** robertscottfacilities@gmail.com
Subject: **I May Be Your Next Facilities Manager**
Date: June 7, 2017
To: **Randy Madden,** randy.madden@slaterfields.com

Hey, Randy —

I just wanted to send a quick note to congratulate you on the tremendous growth that Slater Fields has been experiencing. There must be quite a bit of excitement and chaos around keeping operations running smoothly in the building.

Trust me, I know firsthand how demanding and overwhelming it can be to keep facilities clean, organized, safe, and running smoothly during a period of rapid growth. Perhaps I may be able to support you in keeping day-to-day facility operations afloat as you undergo this inevitably hectic time.

I was faced with a similar situation at Duke Connections. I was their Assistant Facilities Manager and received multiple departmental awards for maintaining the highest levels of overall safety, cleanliness, and building aesthetics—all while supporting the business expansion into 3 new facilities over 18 months.

Anyway, I'm hoping we can talk more at some point this week. Please feel free to reach out to me as I'd love to learn more about your challenges and how I can help you maintain your sanity as Slater Fields continues to grow.

Best —

Robert Scott
356-985-1110
www.linkedin.com/in/rscottfacilities
robertscottfacilities@gmail.com

P.S. I attached my resume so you can read about my background in the Facilities field.

The informal tone of this e-note is appropriate because the job seeker is writing to someone he knows. In a quite concise presentation, he makes a strong case for his value in the precise situation that the company is facing and positions himself well as the solution to their inevitable challenges.

Melanie Denny, MBA • Resume-Evolution • www.resume-evolution.com

From: **Patricia Clark,** clark.patricia@yahoo.com
Subject: **Online Teaching Position with Phoenix University**
Date: May 13, 2017
To: **Helen Brown,** helen.brown@phoenix.edu

As an online educator, I can teach just as competently online as in the traditional classroom. In fact, I have so many more resources available that I'm able to strengthen my courses, expand curricula, create tech-based instructional materials, and further engage my students. The results speak for themselves with improved student grades and overall academic performance.

In addition to teaching, I have years of experience in educational administration, enrollment management, student retention, accreditation, and other functions essential to the effective operation of both online and traditional colleges and universities.

I also have solid academic credentials myself; most significantly, I'm completing my Ph.D. (Industrial & Organizational Psychology) and have earned my MBA (International Business) and BS (Business Management). I've excelled as a student with strong GPAs that always put me in the top of my classes.

My love for teaching and online education positions me as a well-qualified candidate with Phoenix University. I look forward to scheduling an interview, demonstrating my excellence, and becoming a member of your faculty.

Thank you,

Patricia Clark
~~~~~~~~~~~~~~~~~
clark.patricia@yahoo.com
203-345-6789
LinkedIn.com/in/patriciaclark

Attachment: Resume

This letter begins with an observation that is sure to interest institutions that are looking for online educators as that industry grows explosively. Written as an e-note, the letter contains all of the essential skills and keywords relevant to online teaching.

Wendy Enelow, MRW, CCM, JCTC, CPRW • Enelow Executive Career Services • www.wendyenelow.com

INTERIOR DESIGNER
LISA J. THOMPSON

250.989.2354 | British Columbia | LJTDesigner@gmail.com

February 27, 2017

Mr. Robin Scott
BC Designers
1634 Broadway Street
Nanaimo, BC V9T, Canada

Dear Mr. Scott:

It can be difficult for customers to express what they want. By using visuals and over-communicating, I help transform a customer's dreams into reality.

With years of experience, I know how to effectively manage budgetary constraints, plan projects, mitigate design issues, and turn chaos into beautiful spaces. I have a reputation as a positive team player who leads with contagious passion and delivers high-quality results. Here is a glimpse of some of my contributions:

- Expanded customer base 55% at Sutherland Designs by creating do-it-yourself workshops to engage customers in product options and educate them on design possibilities.

- Hired and developed 6 designers for Empire Interiors by sharing retail knowledge, helping with design projects, providing sales techniques, and communicating clear team goals.

- Increased revenue $73,000 (17%) annually at Sutherland Designs by creating unique customer product offerings, developing trusting relationships, and building supplier networks.

With a creative approach that engages customers while generating revenue, I provide outstanding solutions and functional designs. I know that it would be beneficial for us to meet to discuss your needs, and I will call early next week in hopes of scheduling a meeting.

Sincerely,

Lisa J. Thompson

Enclosure: Resume

Enhanced with photographic evidence of this designer's skills, the letter is strong and concise. The 3 bullet points share specific examples—with strong and specific numbers—of her value and contributions. Notice the call to action in the closing paragraph.

Ruth Pankratz, MRW, NCRW, CPRW • Gabby Communications • http://www.gabbycommunications.com

Sara J. Alexander

⊕ sarajalexanderanimation.com
✉ sarajalexander@email.com ☎ 212.870.1234
New York, NY

Motion Graphics Designer + Video Editor

April 26, 2017

James Ellis, Art Director
Larkspur Media
123 3rd Avenue, Suite 8A
New York, NY 10011

Dear Mr. Ellis:

"Sara can fix anything."

I hear this frequently around the Netherfield Marketing offices—from the production team after a difficult shoot, from clients struggling to make an idea they believe in come alive visually, and from executive leadership when a multimillion-dollar project is on the line. I enjoy the challenge of living up to these words every day.

As an **award-winning animator with 8+ years of experience in corporate, boutique, and start-up environments**, I have earned a reputation for conceptualizing and realizing high-quality digital marketing materials across platforms and on tight deadlines. My door is always open to colleagues seeking creative input—and you can often find me in my office after hours helping a junior designer master a new technique.

But results speak louder than words:

▶ I earned a **promotion my first week on the job** after introducing a technique that **saved a $2M project** in jeopardy of missing a critical delivery deadline.

▶ Executive leadership regularly trusts me to lead motion design projects for their most valuable, high-visibility accounts, including **Subaru, Verizon,** and **Showtime Network.**

▶ Recently I salvaged what could have been a disastrous and costly ad re-shoot and turned it into a **viral video** that won client praise and garnered positive **exposure on several national talk shows**.

I love working in a profession that requires constant personal and artistic evolution to stay ahead of the curve. Knowing Larkspur's reputation for cutting-edge design, I believe my aesthetic would be a great fit. I am eager to learn more about your vision and how I can help your creative team take your clients' brands to the next level through innovative visual storytelling. May we set up a time to meet?

Sincerely,

Sara J. Alexander

Both the design and the content of this letter communicate that Sara is a top talent in the field of video animation. She shares both anecdotes and hard facts to paint a picture of a valuable employee. In the last paragraph, notice how she makes a direct connection to the company she's approaching.

Jennifer Fishberg, Ed.M., CPRW, CEIC • Career Karma • www.careerkarma.net

From: **Scott McLaren,** scottmclaren@gmail.com
Subject: **IT Manager—Cisco Expert**
Date: May 1, 2017
To: **Julie Barrowitz,** julie.barrowitz@ITS.com

Ms. Barrowitz—

After 10 years in progressive IT leadership roles, I am seeking a new challenge now that my employer, INNON, is moving away from Cisco. Knowing that ITS is a Cisco partner, I believe that challenge may exist at your company.

A brief summary of my value to ITS:

- **WORKED WITH A WIDE VARIETY OF CISCO TOOLS:** CSCC, CCW, PMC, PPE, PSS, and PPI.

- **CAPTURED MEASURABLE RESULTS:** Cut costs by $800K+ per year, reduced accuracy errors by 60%, and brought in $15M in previously lost rebate money.

- **BUILT AND MENTORED HIGH-TALENT TEAMS:** Created IT department from the ground up in my current position, hiring 22 onshore and 8 offshore professionals. In the role prior to that, I overhauled the department and trained new team members.

- **WON RECOGNITION AND AWARDS:** INNON Award for Outstanding Service (2013, 2014, 2015) and President's Club in 2016.

As a manager, I have focused on creating excellent team environments centered around open communication. I keep the atmosphere light and the accountability high, encouraging my staff to learn rather than simply managing or directing actions.

I look forward to speaking with you to explore the possibility of my joining ITS. With that goal in mind, I will follow up with a phone call early next week. Thank you.

Sincerely,

Scott McLaren
…………………………………………

303-803-0949
scottmclaren@gmail.com
linkedin.com/in/scottmclaren
Denver, CO

Resume attached

Immediately sharing "why I'm writing," this job seeker goes on to provide compelling evidence of knowledge and achievements that position him as a great candidate for this particular company. Notice the subject line that conveys specific expertise relevant to this employer.

Laura Gonzalez, ACRW, CPRW • Masterwork Resumes • www.masterworkresumes.com

Sheldon Cooper, PMP

sheldoncooper07@gmail.com | 513.867.5309 | Milford, OH

Process Improvement Leader | Implementation Manager | ERP Consultant

Methodical project leader, leveraging **PMP** certification, **Six Sigma** Green Belt, and **MBA** in Process Improvement
to enhance internal processes and yield 7-figure savings at major corporations.

April 12, 2017

Jane Williams
Hiring Consultant
Petemore Business Systems
8508 Sycamore Ave
Cincinnati, OH 45208

"… one the best Project Managers with whom I've ever worked …"

"His ability to handle large-scale projects was something on which I could always rely …"

"An A+ hire for any organization …"

In the simplest of terms, the reason others speak so highly of my work is my intense passion for doing things <u>the right way</u>.

Because of this approach, I have seamlessly executed numerous process improvement initiatives that produced substantial results for major corporations. Please consider the results of some notable projects I've led:

- Deployed a $150K ERP system that standardized accounting, time/expense, and payroll systems. I earned recognition for completing this very involved, 3-phased project in less than 6 months and under budget.
- Spearheaded the workforce planning strategy during a major corporate restructuring at MTN. My plan chopped annual labor expenses by $180K without compromising productivity levels.
- Launched comprehensive CRM tool for technical writing team at LexisNexis, yielding annual net gains of $50K.

These are the type of projects (and results) I thrive on, and that is why I would love the opportunity to explore how I can help Petemore Business Systems achieve similar cost savings while maximizing internal efficiencies.

I invite you to review my enclosed resume, which details my work history and further outlines my career achievements, as I am confident I can add value to your team.

Feel free to contact me to set up an interview at your earliest convenience. Thank you for your time and consideration.

Sincerely,

Sheldon Cooper

Three powerful endorsements capture instant attention at the top of this letter. Other notable elements are the headline and branding statement that provide a capsule view of an accomplished project manager. Finally, 3 bullet points are specific examples of value to past employers, indicating what he can do for his next company.

Melanie Denny, MBA • Resume-Evolution • www.resume-evolution.com

From: **Zhara Tomidy,** zhara@zharatomidy.com
Subject: **Can I help grow BitPay's customer base?**
Date: June 14, 2017
To: **Kristina Betts,** kristina.betts@bitpay.com

Hi Kristina,

When I heard that BitPay was having trouble finding product-market fit, I knew I wanted to get involved as soon as possible.

ChangeTip faced a similar challenge last March, so I helped them create a strategic buyer list and led introductions that secured the company a $12M acquisition offer by the beginning of May.

if your customer base is still an area where you're looking to grow, I'd like to share more about how I can deliver similar results for your team.

Best,

Zhara

Zhara Tomidy
Business Development Specialist
248-681-5542 | ZharaTomidy.com | zhara@zharatomidy.com
Twitter: @zharatomidy

Concise, to the point, and all about value: That's the beauty of this e-note. It is a message that is certain to be noticed, read, and remembered, and the example offered is extremely relevant to the "trouble" identified in the opening paragraph. Note the subject line, certain to pique the reader's interest.

Erica Breuer, CPS • Cake Resumes • www.cakeresumes.com

ISABELLA POWERS

Madison, WI ▪ isabella.powers@gmail.com ▪ 608-345-6789

High-level client service and legally trained professional with diverse value-added skillset
CUSTOMER SERVICE | MARKETING | LEGAL AFFAIRS | ADMINISTRATION

March 31, 2017

Martin Alexander
Alexander & Tomlinson, Inc.
2265 Armistead Lane
Los Angeles, CA 90988

Dear Mr. Alexander:

May I bring my commitment to **legendary customer service** to Alexander & Tomlinson—and to your clients?

My career has focused on delivering customer excellence for some of the most prominent law firms in the Midwest. Most notably, I have managed customer relationships that contributed to **year-over-year increases in firm profitability** by managing client capture, engagement, communications, and retention. I believe those functions are the foundation for every successful client-facing organization.

Let me share a few of my achievements I believe to be relevant to Alexander & Tomlinson:

- **Promoted 4 times in 8 years** through increasingly responsible client service and management positions, earning a reputation for "always surpassing objectives" and "exceeding client expectations."

- Demonstrated exceptional marketing talents—**designing** annual marketing kits, **writing** product marketing materials, **creating** client outreach campaigns, and **executing** VIP events.

- Strategically handled **crisis communications** on behalf of the firm and several of its major clients— including large technology firms, a good match for your client specialization at Alexander & Tomlinson.

Complementing my professional experience, I have a BS in marketing and communications and recently earned my **paralegal certification** from an ABA-approved program. Also, I am **bilingual** (English/Spanish).

I would like the opportunity to convince you that I am a perfect addition to your client relationship management team. I will telephone early next week to schedule a convenient time to meet. Thank you.

Sincerely,

Isabella Powers

Resume attached

An attractive heading quickly establishes "who" this job seeker is, and the letter goes on to provide meaningful details of experience and achievement that should definitely interest the reader. Bold type is used throughout the letter to emphasize key points, qualifications, and achievements.

Kristin Johnson, CJSS, CCMC, CARW, COPNS • Profession Director Career Services • www.professiondirection.com

Kansas City, MO 64155 • 816-829-5679 • lsaundersrx@gmail.com

LINDA SAUNDERS, PHARM.D.

June 20, 2017

Ms. Karen Hall
Pharmacy Director
Care Plan
2458 Gilliam
Kansas City, MO 64138

Dear Ms. Hall:

As a well-regarded Pharmacist with broad-based experience and a service-oriented approach, I offer a set of skills that would make me a welcome and valuable addition to your staff. I would like to put my knowledge and experience to work for Care Plan as a Staff Pharmacist.

As you can see from my attached resume, I bring a record of accomplishment in a variety of settings—hospital, clinical, and retail pharmacies. In my career, I have built a reputation as a team player who goes "above and beyond" in providing support and customer service. My track record reflects:

- A strong ability and commitment to dispensing drugs **safely and efficiently.**
- A sound understanding of the **principles underlying pharmaceutical care.**
- Vigilance in recognizing **therapeutic incompatibilities.**
- Proactive leadership in the development, implementation, and analysis of **disease-management programs.**

I am eager to share my commitment to making a difference in patients' lives and don't think you will find a more motivated or enthusiastic Pharmacist. I would welcome the opportunity to discuss mutual interests and how my skills may benefit your organization. Please let me know what time would be suitable for you. I can be reached by phone (816-829-5679) or email (lsaundersrx@gmail.com).

Sincerely,

Linda Saunders

Enclosure: Resume

> The attractive mortar-and-pestle graphic instantly communicates "I am a pharmacist." The bullet points that are the focal point of the letter's content highlight 4 specific skills that are essential for success in the field. Finally, the letter also references soft skills that are valuable for anyone working in healthcare and serving the public.

Andrea Adamski, CPRW • Write for You Resumes • www.writeforyoukc.com

MARY NOLAN

marynolan@yahoo.com | 912-252-1034 | in

SENIOR FIELD MARKETING EXECUTIVE
RETAIL OPERATIONS – TRADE MARKETING – SHOPPER-CENTRIC STRATEGIES
◆ ◆ ◆

March 1, 2017

Ms. Karen McCarthy
Human Resources Manager
Goodyear Tire & Rubber Company
21991 Brecksville Road
Brecksville, OH 44144

Dear Ms. McCarthy:

"What I've appreciated about Mary is her collaborative approach to gain buy-in from clients … She is passionate about her work, is a driver, and doesn't take 'no' for an answer."

-- Todd Parker, Michelin Sales Manager for McGriber Tire (Independent Dealer)

As a retail marketing leader, I am known for driving sales and increasing market share through a multi-channel approach. I work tirelessly to develop rapport with clients, earning their trust with data-driven strategies.

In brief, I am a proven performer with broad expertise in sales, marketing, and brand management in the automotive aftermarket, entertainment, sports, and beverage industries. My history includes:

♦ 180% increase in ROI for targeted retailers focused on print campaigns.
♦ 7% uptick in private-label credit-card sales despite reduction in retailers (12% fewer stores).
♦ 2.7% improvement in conversion rate with rollout of new database marketing program.

Promoted rapidly during my tenure with one of America's most respected companies, I am quite secure in my position. However, I'm ready for a change … ready for new opportunities and new challenges. As such, I am confidently exploring senior-level field marketing positions and would welcome the opportunity for a personal interview. I will follow up next week to schedule a time that is convenient. Thank you.

Sincerely,

Mary Nolan

Enclosure: resume

A third-party endorsement is a great attention-getter at the start of a letter that is concisely written yet includes a great deal of relevant information. Note the assertive follow-up in the closing paragraph. The header at the top matches the resume, creating an attractive and cohesive package.

Kris McGuigan, ACRW, CCMC • Professional Courage LLC • professionalcourage.com

CORBIN WASHINGTON

344-321-4242 - Chicago, IL - corbinw500@gmail.com

VP SALES
Enterprise Technology & Strategic Alliances

Millions in Revenue Opportunities & Strategic Deals at Emerging Technology Firms

March 23, 2017

Dean Jones
Northfield Social Management, Inc.
10 N. Newbern Avenue
Denver, CO 80223

Dear Mr. Jones:

As a Strategic Sales Director and VP Strategic Partnerships credited with revitalizing sales practices—***resulting in deals exceeding the norm by 300% and generating $55M+ in a challenged market***—I'm laser-focused on new revenue opportunities and innovation in the tech arena.

I can bring this focus, this leadership, and these results to Northfield Social Management.

Examples of my leadership and results in <u>aggressive software and IT solutions markets</u> (ERP, CRM, commerce, systems, e-procurement, and other products) include:

> **Numerous first-time performance benchmarks** in company history, including the largest company sale, a new partnership with IBM Marketing Cloud, and the #1 upselling contract (**50%** higher vs. other deals);
>
> **More than 1,000-fold growth in TCV** for SocialWorx by orchestrating a switch to multi-year agreements and repeatedly proving the value of our solutions at Fortune-ranked companies;
>
> **High-volume sales activity,** as evidenced by marketing and sales of more than 300 units at Conway Advisors, where I hired teams and brokers generating **$55M.**

Committed to growing your revenues, I'm also able to build a sharp, focused team from the ground up, ensuring a strong demonstration of business value to your customers.

To explore possibilities, I will follow up in the next few days.

Sincerely,

Corbin Washington

The design of this letter is both attractive and functional: It calls attention to the job seeker's core expertise (in the header) and most notable achievements (in the 3 indented statements). Bold type throughout further emphasizes key numbers and results that demonstrate his expertise in both sales and technology.

Laura Smith-Proulx, CCMC, CPRW, CTTCC, CPBA, TCCS, COPNS • An Expert Resume • www.anexpertresume.com

From: **Frank Reagan,** frankreagan@mac.com
Subject: **Finance & Technology Executive**
Date: February 7, 2017
To: **Alexander Kern,** alexkern@globalco.com

The attached resume tells the story of my 17-year career bringing cost-conscious leadership to the financial function of complex multinational companies like yours.

The scope of my expertise includes the full range of corporate finance, accounting, budgeting, regulatory affairs, and investment management, but it's how I leverage the latest in technology that would provide the most value to your organization. My greatest strength is identifying IT opportunities that cross geographic boundaries to streamline financial information, remove redundancies, and slash costs.

A few of my career highlights:

- Spearheaded the acquisition and smooth **financial system integration of a $150M manufacturing company**.
- Restructured **12** company-wide finance-related systems, from full network conversions to accounting system upgrades and automated vendor payment tracking.
- Introduced payroll direct deposit across **6 countries** and **5 currencies, saving an average $25K** in annual costs and **achieving 90% employee participation** during the first 5 months of rollout.

I have consistently delivered strong performance results through my contributions to internal controls and technology solutions that add to the bottom line and minimize risk. If you're hoping to spark both profitability and productivity, I'll blend technical and financial functions to deliver the highest standard in financial management.

I would welcome an opportunity to discuss my credentials in person.

Sincerely,

Frank Reagan
===========================
555-660-9081
frankreagan@mac.com
linkedin.com/in/frankreagan

Clearly and concisely written, this letter packs a lot of information and relevant keywords into a very tidy package. Most notable are the 3 bullet points, true "career highlights" that illustrate the job seeker's skills, achievements, and value as they relate directly to the targeted company.

Emily Wong, MIM, ACRW, CPRW • Words of Distinction • www.wordsofdistinction.net

From:	**Steven Pearson,** stevenpearson@gmail.com
Subject:	**Turning Around and Driving Sales Results for Your Company**
Date:	April 3, 2017
To:	**Estella Ortiz,** e.ortiz@excelnetworks.com

Ms. Ortiz,

As a COO, I have repeatedly shown that I can revitalize underperforming businesses, close deals considered impossible, win long-term customer loyalty, and lead organizations to the next level of growth.

I have created and executed revenue-generating strategies for both global Fortune 500 and VC-backed software companies, delivering results like these:

- **Growing the business 25% to $350M in one year** at Sorrenson Enterprises and **increasing revenues from $40M to $500M in 3 years** at Kline Corporation.

- Building Hewitt Solutions' North American operations **from $0 to $78M in one year.**

- **Achieving 98% customer satisfaction** and leading team to develop a reference database of 2000 top Fortune customers at Drake Corporation.

- **Delivering division and region turnarounds** at Sorrenson Enterprises and Kline Corporation and leading the **seamless integration of acquisitions,** including a multibillion-dollar company.

When I joined Sorrenson as COO of its largest division, the organization was losing significant market share and sales—no new business generated in 16 months. I restored it to profitability in 12 months and tripled revenues.

Now that I have laid the foundation for a successful division, I am ready to take on a new business challenge where I can make an immediate contribution to revenue growth. May we meet to discuss the value I will bring to Excel Networks?

Sincerely,

Steven Pearson
****
974-668-1220
stevenpearson@gmail.com
LinkedIn.com/in/StevenPearson

Packed with impressive results, this e-note comes right to the point and remains sharply focused throughout. The bullet points are highlighted with bold print that calls attention to numbers and results. Also notice how this job seeker explains the reason for his search since he is still employed—a big plus in job search.

Louise Garver, CERM, CPRW, CJSS, CPBS • Career Directions, LLC • https://careerdirectionsllc.com

SARAH C. FRESNETH – OPERATIONS MANAGEMENT

276-365-9870 | Sarah.Fresneth@gmail.com

PROCESS DEVELOPMENT | PROJECT MANAGEMENT | LARGE-SCALE PROJECT PLANNING
❈ ❈ ❈ Matrix Environments: Manufacturing, Distribution, Production, Defense ❈ ❈ ❈

January 5, 2017

Christopher Nez
Vice President of Expansion
Dunlop Shipping Corporation
11001 Waterway Plaza
Coastal Plains, AK 99504

Dear Mr. Nez:

Reading about Dunlop's international expansion objectives in the *Anchorage Business Courier,* it occurred to me that you may be looking to augment your management team.

For the last several years, I supervised lean production and manufacturing operations for an industrial product manufacturing company. In this role, I reduced waste, optimized human capital, and increased the efficiency of shipping operations by 200%, in record time (less than 90 days).

Prior to managing projects in the corporate world, I served as a Commissioned Officer with the Department of Defense, where I led division-level operations supporting training, transportation, logistics, and communications in both domestic and international arenas.

I am ready to travel, willing to negotiate, and prepared to make a firm commitment to driving future growth and profits for Dunlop.

When we meet, I plan to outline the immediate value my knowledge, network, and experience will bring in helping you reach your expansion goals.

Sincerely,

Sarah Fresneth

P.S. In addition to an MS in International Communications, I offer numerous credentials in project management, backed with a keen understanding of fiduciary responsibility in managing multimillion-dollar budgets.

Making an immediate connection, this letter opens with a reference to a newspaper article about the company that the candidate just read. It goes on to present valuable information in short, easy-to-skim paragraphs. The heading at the top is also quite valuable in immediately defining this job seeker's areas of expertise.

Lisa Parker, CERM, CPRW, CEIP • Professional Resume Presentations • www.parkercprw.com

From: **John Yelanjian,** johnyelanjian@ymail.com
Subject: **Construction Executive**
Date: June 14, 2017
To: **Info@SmithfieldConstruction.com**

"His work ethic, temperament, and leadership skills are met by his gifts and knowledge. Able and enthusiastic, he owns my full trust." – James Landers, Landers Pennington Architecture

I am a highly experienced builder and project manager with a 15-year portfolio of distinctive, high-end homes and a Bachelor of Science in Construction Management. My nationally recognized work has been featured in *Architectural Digest, Southern Living,* and *Southern Accents.*

Because my goal is to maintain superb quality and workmanship, I personally keep a close eye on all phases of the job, motivating employees and challenging contractors to achieve/surpass quality objectives on schedule and within budget. Providing clear direction and exhibiting mutual respect, I develop employees who have high standards and move up quickly in their field of work.

If you need an executive project manager with an established portfolio of one-of-a-kind projects and a reputation for excellence, I hope you will give me a call. I would like to talk with you about how I can contribute to your company's profitability and help you create memorable living spaces.

John Yelanjian

Cell: (404) 555-1212
Email: johnyelanjian@ymail.com
LinkedIn: www.linkedin.com/in/johnyelanjian
Facebook: www.facebook.com/superbconstruction

Attachment: Resume

A stellar endorsement, an overview of experience and awards, and a few sentences about leadership style—in just 4 short paragraphs, this e-note conveys a great deal of critical information. Because it not addressed to a specific individual, the closing is written appropriately to invite a call.

Alexia Scott, CPRW • A Winning Resume • www.a-winning-resume.com

Nina M. Summers, RN, MBA-HCA, FACHE

(313) 652-1334   linkedin.com/in/ninamsummers   nmsummers@gmail.com

March 30, 2017

Mr. Kenneth Stokes, Director of Human Resources
Rush University Medical Center
1653 W Congress Pkwy
Chicago, IL 60612

Dear Mr. Stokes:

As a healthcare executive, I am known as a change agent—creating culture, clarifying vision, and managing resources to drive performance across the spectrum of service, quality, and affordability.

The attached resume describes my tenure with one of the nation's leading healthcare systems, during which I advanced to increasingly responsible leadership roles. Recent accomplishments include:

- **Executive Leadership:** Established learning culture throughout the organization with full assessment and restructure of leadership skill set from the top down. Stepped up to make difficult transitions where needed.

- **Quality Redesign:** Drove patient safety initiatives, implementing daily huddles and patient experience rounding. Secured board representation on the Quality Committee. Achieved consistency of practice, decreased mortality 23%, and reduced length of stay by 3 days.

- **System Integration:** Executed action plans to realign practices to the mission of driving wellness within the community. Realized gains in market share (43% surgical and 25% ancillary services), drove physician recruitment, and improved patient satisfaction scores by 17 points.

- **Profitability:** Challenged team to identify waste and improve efficiency. Yielded $2.5M in recovery dollars in 4 distinct areas.

Recently recognized by *Crain's Chicago Business* as a 2017 Woman of Note, I bring a balance of talent and tenacity to create change and improve service within the healthcare arena.

If your institution seeks a top performer who can navigate the rapidly changing marketplace to deliver service excellence, I would welcome the opportunity to meet with you.

Sincerely,

Nina M. Summers

> Bold headings introduce 4 strong bullet points that provide specific examples of leadership and results for this executive, and the following paragraph showcases a distinguishing honor. All content is crisply written to make this letter highly readable.

Kris McGuigan, ACRW, CCMC • Professional Courage LLC • professionalcourage.com

GLOBAL TECHNOLOGY & BUSINESS DEVELOPMENT LEADER
► *CTO for $4.9B Business* ◄ ► *$80M Enterprise Account Strategist* ◄

513.929.5924 ▪ malinda.s.hillyer@outlook.com ▪ linkedin.com/in/malindahillyer ▪ Cincinnati, OH 45209

March 20, 2017

Erika Palmer
Hindera Group
342 Oakwood Dr., Ste. 800
Cincinnati, OH 45226

Dear Ms. Palmer:

If you are looking for a **Senior Technology Executive** with game-changing influence on business, operations, and technology performance, you may be interested in my background and impact in these areas. Here is what I offer:

Maximum ROI via Technology Strategy: Adept at seizing new opportunities, I regularly chair conversations with company leaders to ensure future growth through strategic technology development and investment initiatives.

☑ Paved the way for **10% market share growth** and **$15M annual revenue gain** as current CTO of a $4.9B business, leading due diligence on a key M&A project and introducing Big Data / IoT strategy.

Exponential Growth through Diverse Expertise: With extensive insight to the $606B software services and $177B automation markets—along with operations management and business development acumen—I have delivered impressive, long-lasting results both for my companies and for major B2B customers.

☑ **Tripled business growth** and **increased project margins 13%+ in 4 years** as Business Unit Manager at Rickwell Automation by overhauling an outdated business model and adding professional services.

Revenue Upsurge with Ingenuity & Relationship Building: By cultivating influencer relationships and solving technology issues, I have positioned my companies to unseat long-standing competitors from high-value accounts.

☑ **Grew territory 450% with 156 new customers** and master-planned compelling bid to **win $8M/year Dow Corning contract** at Siemens. Later saved GM account and **fueled $25M in annual revenues.**

Technology and business development initiatives aren't the only hallmarks of my career. Just as critical, my dedication to ongoing learning—for personal and team development—has increased our competitive edge.

You'll find further proof of my impact on the attached resume. I would appreciate a discovery session to explore opportunities and will be in touch Wednesday to set up a time for a chat.

Sincerely,

Malinda S. Hillyer
Attached: Resume

> This well-designed letter leads the reader from general capabilities to specific achievements that are highlighted in bold in each bullet point. In all, the letter paints a solid portrait of a capable, accomplished, and dedicated executive. Note the assertive closing that keeps follow-up in the job seeker's hands—not the employer's.

Sandra Ingemansen, CERM, CMRW, CPRW, CJSS • Resume Strategies • www.resume-strategies.com

From: **Pierre Rondeau,** pierre.rondeau@mac.com
Subject: **European Sales Leadership: V-Chip, TechStars, Panasonic**
Date: June 14, 2017
To: **Tanya Yakamura,** tanya.yakamura@hitech.com

Ms. Yakamura:

With more than 12 years of success building French and European business for world leaders V-Chip, TechStars, and Panasonic, I have the expertise that grows sales, drives profits, and strengthens an organization's bottom line.

My value can best be illustrated by the following challenges and results:

V-CHIP

- *Challenge:* Restructure marketing and sales in southern Europe post-merger, integrating 2 distinct corporate cultures.
- *Results:* Built an efficient, high-performing organization with a true teamwork mentality. Achieved 30% sales growth and maintained market share above 50% in all 3 product sectors.

TECHSTARS

- *Challenge:* Meet high revenue objectives in a sales department that grew from 4 to 35 and targeted business in 3 distinct channels: resellers, VARs, and corporate accounts.
- *Results:* Increased sales from nearly zero to $30M and won more than 100,000 contracts.

PANASONIC

- *Challenge:* Gain market share in France with a virtually unknown line of products.
- *Results:* In 3 years, led a 4-member sales team in generating more than $18M annual revenue.

I look forward to bringing this same level of professionalism and results to your organization—whether you seek a country/branch manager to lead the entire French organization, or a seasoned sales/marketing executive who can create and execute strategies for France and Europe. I would appreciate the opportunity to discuss how I can meet (and exceed) your expectations.

Sincerely,

Pierre Rondeau

+33 6 04 35 1254
pierre.rondeau@mac.com
LinkedIn profile

Resume attached

Identifying specific sales-related challenges and distinct results for 3 different companies, this e-note clearly makes the point that the job seeker is tops in sales in France and throughout Europe—where he wants to continue working. The content is tightly written and the format is easy to skim.

Louise Kursmark, MRW, CPRW, CCM, JCTC, CEIP • Best Impression Career Services • www.louisekursmark.com

From: **Mike Kulturni,** mkulturni@me.com
Subject: **Senior Executive Behind MullerCoors' Rapid, Value-Creating Growth**
Date: March 15, 2017
To: **Frank O'Hara,** ohara.frank@abcbeer

Good morning, Frank:

Are you in search of a proven leader who can orchestrate peak value from strategy, operations, and technology?

With large mainstream CPG and F&B brands facing cutthroat competition at every turn, pivoting strategy, operations, and company culture is necessary to stay in demand. As ABC Beers now faces real threats from 2 industry disruptors, you may be interested in my successes with **SABMuller, MullerCours,** and **Enilever:**

➔ Serving on the strategic leadership team that **turned around** Muller Brewing Company and **propelled global business to $4.9B** within 3 short years.

➔ Writing the business case that **formed the $7.0B MullerCoors** JV in 2007; then leading post-acquisition integration and cost synergies that were critical to **saving $765M.**

➔ **Transforming Enilever's largest CPG factory in the Southern Hemisphere** while creating equality for a 300-person workforce in turbulent pre-democratic South Africa—and **saving $60M** in the process.

I would appreciate a confidential discussion to talk about how I can contribute to ABC Beer's sustained success in a senior management role. Let's set up a time next week to chat.

Mike Kulturni

Mobile: +1.414.967.4283
Email: mkulturni@me.com

~~~~~~~~~~~~~~~~~~~~

Attachment: Resume

P.S. You can learn more about my leadership experience here: http://www.linkedin.com/in/michaelkulturni.

This short e-note packs a punch by asking a question at the very beginning to capture the reader's interest, then sharing 4 notable achievements directly on target with what the company needs as it strives to maintain its strong market position. The P.S. is always a nice addition—and almost always gets read.

CHAPTER 4:
Recruiter Letters

What Is a Recruiter Letter?

Recruiter letters are job search letters sent to recruiters, executive search firms, and other third parties that place external candidates into companies. You will use recruiter letters in 2 instances:

- In response to an advertised job posting from the recruiter.

- As a cold call introduction to explore job opportunities that the recruiter may be trying to fill on behalf of the companies that he represents.

Recruiter letters are often quite similar to job posting letters (Chapter 2) and cold call letters (Chapter 3). Like those letters, they also showcase your skills, experience, education, achievements, and other talents that make you uniquely qualified for the positions you're targeting.

However, recruiter letters may also feature information that you would *not* share with a company at this early stage in the interviewing and hiring process. Read on as we explain.

What Do You Want to Achieve in Your Recruiter Letter?

When writing to a recruiter *in response to a job posting,* you want to position yourself as the #1 candidate. You achieve this by prominently showcasing your qualifications and matching them to the job posting.

When writing a *cold call letter* to a recruiter, your goal is the same—to demonstrate that you are a well-qualified candidate for positions that may arise in the future. That creates a unique challenge because you don't have a listing of required qualifications to guide your letter writing.

In that situation, engage the recruiter by immediately sharing information that you believe is relevant to the positions and industries in which she specializes. You have about 5 seconds to capture someone's interest, so make it count with strong and memorable content. The next section in this chapter discusses letter content in detail.

You want your cold call letter to prompt one of these 4 actions:

- A phone call or email message telling you about a job posting that you were not aware of.

- A phone call or email message for a position that has not been posted.

- A referral to another recruiter who has a search for a candidate with your qualifications.

- Inclusion of your letter and resume in the recruiter's candidate database for future consideration. Although it's rare to get a call back, it does happen! Increase your chances by focusing on the right recruiters—ones who specialize in the profession(s) and industry(ies) in which you have experience.

> **Pro Tip: Recruiters are not known for being out-of-the-box thinkers.** Even though you might consider your experience as a chemical engineer easily transferrable to a position in manufacturing, that's not what the recruiter's client company has asked for, and therefore you will generally not be considered.
>
> But don't take it personally. Understand that the recruiter is compensated by a hiring company that is looking for a specific skill/experience mix. The recruiter's job is to find great candidates that fit the bill—*not* to find a job for you. If you are a well-qualified candidate according to the hiring company's criteria, you'll find the recruiter is a helpful partner in your job search. Accept the reality, understand what drives the recruiter, and don't expect a recruiter to do your job search work for you.

How Do You Write a Recruiter Letter?

If you are writing a recruiter letter in response to a job posting, it's just about as easy as writing directly to a company in response to one of its advertisements. Write a letter that clearly demonstrates that you have the skills, experiences, educational credentials, and other requirements described in the job posting.

With a cold call recruiter letter, you must make an instant connection with the recruiter by closely aligning your career experience with the specific industries and professions in which that recruiter specializes.

Here are 3 tips that we consider to be the most important when writing to recruiting firms:

- **Customize to each job posting or recruiter specialization.** Of course, if you are applying for multiple positions that require similar skills and experience, it won't take long to customize each letter. Just be certain to prominently mention your qualifications that match the core requirements of the advertised opportunity—or that match what you know about that recruiter's niche expertise.

- **Be unique, memorable, distinctive, and competitive.** This is true whether writing in response to a recruiter job posting or sending a cold call letter. You give yourself an immediate advantage when you communicate that you bring a unique set of skills and memorable achievements; when you share distinguishing information about your experience, education, or performance; or when you demonstrate that you are the most qualified candidate for an opportunity.

- **Use all keywords appropriate for the professions and industries in which that recruiter works.** Almost every recruitment and executive search firm will put your resume through their own keyword-based Applicant Tracking System (ATS). You *must* have the right words to get noticed electronically or you will be passed over. It is that fundamental.

  Be certain to include keywords that represent hard skills. If you are a health care provider, you might include words such as *patient care, patient education, medication administration, charting, and regulatory compliance.* Just as important for that same health care worker are soft skills and attributes such as *compassion, accuracy, dedication, and prioritization.*

As we outlined in Chapter 2, other information can be used in keyword scanning, and many of those extras are out of your control. You don't necessary think of UCLA or USC as keywords, but they can be if a company is looking for a recent college graduate from either of those 2 California-based universities. The same is true for college degrees—BSBA, MBA, BSN. They're essential keywords if they reflect the job requirements.

Similarly, job titles, company names, cities, states, and even zip codes are often used for keyword scanning. If a company wants to hire an experienced chemical engineer, then those exact words—chemical engineer—must be the job title that is read by ATS. It's a matching game in many instances, and it is one of the foundations of today's job search landscape.

So that you're not wasting your time or the recruiter's, don't hesitate to lay all of your cards on the table and include information that you would almost never share with a company at this initial point of contact.

Such information will typically include the first 3 items on the following list and perhaps the other items as well, if relevant to you, your family, and your personal situation:

- Current salary requirements
- Brief mention of salary history
- Specific dates for availability to start a new job
- Geographic requirements, if any
- Citizenship, immigration, or right-to-work status, if relevant
- Special family needs for health care, education, and other services
- Personal information that will give a recruiter a broader perception of who you are

How Do You Submit a Recruiter Letter?

As outlined at the beginning of this chapter, you will write a recruiter letter in 2 circumstances: in response to an advertised job posting, or as a cold call introduction to explore current or future opportunities.

The method for submitting your recruiter letter will depend on the situation. You might:

- **Upload your letter** along with your resume—either as 1 combined file (letter and resume) or as 2 separate files. Make that decision based on the specific upload requirements for each posting. If given the option, we suggest uploading PDFs rather than Word files to retain formatting integrity.

  Once you have uploaded your documents, they will need to pass through keyword-based Applicant Tracking Systems (ATS). That is what makes it so imperative to follow the firm's instructions. If your documents don't pass the technology scan, they will never be seen by a human.

- **Email your letter** along with your resume. Paste your letter as an e-note in the body of the email message. Then, attach your resume as a PDF or Word document. Just as when you're uploading, our recommendation is to use PDF files whenever possible to retain formatting integrity.

Who Is the Audience?

Obviously, the intended recipients for these letters are recruiters, executive search firms, and other third-party companies that specialize in talent acquisition.

> **Pro Tip: Remember that recruiters do not work for you** … they do not work for individual candidates. They are paid by the companies that hire them to find qualified candidates to fill specific positions.

All too many job seekers expect recruiters to be interested in them, to want to work to place them, and to be on their "side," but that is not the case. Just like any other business, their primary goal is to meet the needs of their clients. Candidates, like yourself, are a great asset to them if you have the right qualifications for a particular search assignment. If not, their interest is elsewhere, and that's understandable.

Realign your expectations, understand how third-party recruitment works, and you'll be much more effective in your search and less frustrated when inquiries to a recruiter go unanswered.

To Whom Do You Send It?

If you're writing a cold call letter to a recruiter, do your research and find the name of a specific individual. Otherwise, chances are good that your message will simply be ignored. Send the letter via email because the recruiter wants your information electronically so it can be stored in his candidate database and ultimately forwarded to the client company.

Fortunately, it's relatively easy to find people's names and their direct contact information. Look on the recruiting firm's website for contact information, search on LinkedIn, and visit the firm's Facebook page or other social media channels they may use.

If you're writing a recruiter letter in response to a job posting, follow the instructions. In some instances, you will upload your letter and resume to the company's website, and other times you will send your material via email. Address the letter to the person or department indicated in the posting.

Why is it so important to find a person's name? When you have a name, you have the power to follow up. Without a name, you are stuck waiting … wishing and hoping for a reply that may never come. When you follow up, you might connect, and you will definitely set yourself apart from other candidates and get the attention of that recruiter. Often that's the most difficult thing to accomplish.

> **Pro Tip: If the job posting does not provide a name, omit the salutation line altogether.** Do not use "To Whom It May Concern," "Dear Sir/Madam," "Dear Recruiter," or any other generic language. Those introductions are dated and no longer necessary.

What Are the Unique Characteristics of a Recruiter Letter?

On the following pages, you will find 10 sample letters that demonstrate a wide variety of ways to write, format, and design recruiter letters. Read the box below each letter to find helpful notes and insights regarding that specific letter.

PETER STRONGHOLD

19 Dorothy Place, Kansas City, MO 64108 ▪ C: 816.543.2255
PeterStronghold@gmail.com ▪ **https://www.linkedin.com/in/peterstrong77**

ENTRY-LEVEL FINANCIAL ANALYST

February 8, 2017

Sandra Mason
Standard Recruiting, Inc.
Kansas City, MO 64105

Dear Ms. Mason:

In exploring financial analyst and accounting opportunities, I am seeking to partner with your agency in finding a position where I can contribute the skills and knowledge gained from my recent BSBA degree and hands-on business experience.

My background demonstrates my ability to multitask in fast-paced, demanding, and tight-deadline settings, while remaining focused and well-informed. In each assignment, I willingly committed time and energy to learn and master statistical tools, software programs, online resources, and company processes. I bring to a financial team my tireless work ethic, self-motivation, and proven record of meeting and accomplishing each challenge.

In assessing my candidacy, please note the following qualifications:

- **Estimated Profit Growth:** Reviewed, analyzed, and synthesized financial data in achieving simulated revenue goals, profit margins, customer satisfaction, and cost savings, achieving #1 class ranking.

- **Business Skills:** Applied careful attention to details, excellent time management, and exceptional organizational abilities in balancing multiple priorities, completing work accurately and thoroughly, and streamlining and improving study and work processes.

- **Team Leadership:** Frequently remained after hours and came in on weekends to mentor other team members and assist in completing group projects. Helped identify potential problems and offered solutions in avoiding inaccurate and incomplete findings.

- **Financial Analysis:** Used education and experience with statistical research, business forecasting, financial modeling, problem solving, and negotiations in benefiting companies in case studies.

Confident that I will become a valued member of one of your client companies, I would like to discuss my credentials in a phone or in-person meeting. Thank you for your attention; I look forward to speaking with you.

Sincerely,

Peter Stronghold

Attachment

The shaded heading instantly identifies this job seeker's target position—extremely helpful information to a recruiter. Notice that many of the qualifications and experiences come from the classroom, as is appropriate for this new graduate, yet he presents them in a professional experience style.

Freddie Cheek, CCM, MCD, CPRW, CARW, CWDP, MS Ed • First Resume Services • www.cheekandassociates.com

CARRIE EASTLEY

E: ceastley@gmail.com
Hobart, TAS 7001

M: 0400 222 333
LinkedIn Profile

> *"A good executive assistant is like an air traffic controller for your life".*
> *MICHAEL HYATT*

04 June 2017

Searson Buck Recruitment
Attention: Rachael Jones

Online Application—Resume Uploaded

RE: Executive Assistant Ref: 65423/RJ

One look at my resume and you'll see that I have the experience it takes to support your client's CEO.

As a high-performing Executive Assistant with 15 years' experience, I have provided high-level, professional executive support in diverse settings. Aligning seamlessly with your client's requirements, I possess:

❖ A proven track record in managing both the personal and professional lives of executives.
❖ Advanced software and computer system skills, including Microsoft Word, Excel, and PowerPoint.
❖ Complex diary management expertise—scheduling and organising meetings, appointments, and travel.
❖ Well-honed events and project management proficiency and the ability to juggle multiple projects.

As the "right hand" to the Finance Director of ComputerXO, I managed the facilities and procurement departments for the head office and 12 subsidiaries. I am known for rolling up my sleeves and pitching in to ensure a project is completed to high professional standards and with the desired results.

My core values are reliability, integrity, team collaboration, and quality in performance.

I am confident that I can deliver real value to your client's organisation and would be delighted to meet in person to discuss my background and achievements. Thank you for your consideration.

Yours sincerely,

Carrie Eastley

All of the skills and experiences detailed in this resume are highly relevant—and matched to the specific details in the position description. At the top, a quote in a shaded box creates interest and answers the "who I am" question quickly and effectively.

Carolyn Whitfield, CERW, CMRW, CARW • carolynwhitfield.flavors.me

From: **Luis Montero,** luis.montero@gmail.com
Subject: **Senior Sales Professional—Pharmaceutical/Medical**
Date: January 23, 2017
To: **Alyssa Roberts,** alyssa.roberts@medsalesspecialists.com

These highlights of my sales successes may be of interest to one of your clients:

- ❖ **200% jump in business in one year in pharmaceutical sales for Pro-Vax.**
- ❖ **130% achievement of strategic business initiatives for medical products provider Health-All.**
- ❖ **Turnaround of a major hospital system account within 3 months.**
- ❖ **Superior results in up and down markets.**

My supervisors look at the bottom line and acknowledge my overall contributions to the company. My clients will tell you that I am:

- ❖ Efficient and organized.
- ❖ Genuinely helpful, with superior follow-through.
- ❖ A natural at building rapport and fostering mutually beneficial relationships.

My passion for healthcare stems from growing up in a household of nurses and clinicians who worked with the elderly, where accurate diagnoses, prescriptions, and dosages are of utmost importance. Although my work is different, I bring this same dedication and attention to detail to everything I do.

I would welcome your call to discuss how I can bring my skills and experience to your client's company. Note that my salary requirements are $85K+ plus bonus and other incentives. I am open to relocation but do have a special-needs child who requires excellent healthcare and educational resources.

Sincerely,

Luis Montero
luis.montero@gmail.com
931-456-1212 [CALL OR TEXT]
LinkedIn.com/in/LuisMontero

Resume attached

The double set of bullet points captures attention—the first set highlighting strong sales results, the second expressing valuable soft skills. This job seeker also briefly adds personal information, in the next-to-last paragraph, that helps the recruiter understand why he is so dedicated to his profession.

Debra Ann Matthews, MA, JCTC, JCDC • Let Me Write It For You • www.letmewriteitforyou.org

From: **Roberta Carver,** rcarver@gmail.com
Subject: **Visual Merchandising Manager Opportunities**
Date: February 23, 2017
To: **JR Jones,** jrjones@retailrecruiters.com

To present me for **Visual Merchandising Manager** positions, you must be confident I can generate <u>AND</u> implement ideas, producing great outcomes for your client's brand.

As a Creative who exercises discipline in design execution, I inspire visual excellence, bringing concepts to fruition while increasing sales and customer attention. I've worked globally for a **$1B** retailer, training workforces and sales teams on the artistry of visual merchandising combined with the right execution.

Visual impact is paramount to brand appeal. It enhances aesthetics of displays, sales floors, and corporate directives with strategically planned visual concepts that shift customer behavior. I've paired these vital visual strategies with lean project management principles to achieve:

➥ Sales gains of **15%** after implementing new concepts affecting product mix and floor displays.
➥ Brand unification and transformation through redefined communication standards.
➥ Optimization of floor space, adding new designers and adjusting visual identity to reflect demand.

I love my job and its power to evoke emotion.

Please review my resume and let's discuss my candidacy for your **Visual Merchandising Manager** positions. I am open to relocation nationwide and would anticipate a compensation package between $95K and $115K. I'll call next week to schedule a meeting.

Best regards,

Roberta Carver
===========
rcarver@gmail.com
(312) 254-3378
www.linkedin.com/in/rcarvervision

** Resume attached to email

This e-note appeals to the needs of both the recruiter *and* the hiring company, describing a blend of professional skills and specific achievements. It includes critical information about salary and relocation and, unlike many recruiter letters, closes on an assertive note with a promise to call.

Kimberly A. Sernel, CPA, ACRW, CPRW • Horizon Career Solutions • www.horizoncareersolutions.com

Randolph Decker

959-555-3406 | rdecker@gmail.com
Hartford, CT | Linkedin.com/in/RandolphDecker

January 10, 2017

James V. Tsai, Managing Partner
Market Encore Associates
55-230 Prentiss Blvd.
Los Angeles, CA 90025

Re: **Regional Sales Management—Telecommunications Industry**

Dear Mr. Tsai:

Do you have a client in need of a regional sales management executive? My 12 years of experience spanning Premiere Telecomm Solutions, Summit Telecommunications Group, and TechCon demonstrates proven success in streamlining operations, driving marketing efforts and sales presentations, and closing deals.

Proven Value:

- Currently at Premiere Telecomm, I work nationwide with more than 300 agents and brokers, supporting their efforts to turn around underperforming territories, restore accounts, and develop new and existing business.
- At Summit Telecommunications, I was a member of the Senior Executive Advisory Committee and maintained top 5% performance ratings no matter what the economic climate.
- At TechCon, I completed a rigorous 6-month Business Leadership and Sales Training Program in the top 3.

Additional Value:

- An enthusiastic and engaging speaker, I have presented to groups of 250 and national sales conferences.
- I've had great success in the tough NYC market and can leverage industry-wide relationships to build, develop, and support a high-performing sales team.

My experience is mainly in telecommunications technology, but I am well qualified to lead any sales team in an organization seeking to achieve market dominance as well as aggressive revenue and profit goals. I am open to relocation anywhere in the country but prefer the East Coast. Expected compensation package: $185K+.

Please contact me at your earliest convenience, as I am prepared to move quickly to my next opportunity.

Sincerely,

Randolph Decker

Attachment

The hallmark of this letter is *clarity*. The job seeker defines who he is, what he's good at, and where and how he has had success. Note the "Additional Value" bullet points—extras that distinguish him from other candidates. Also notice recruiter-appropriate details (geographic location and salary) in the next-to-last paragraph.

Marjorie Sussman, MRW, ACRW • www.visualcv.com/marjoriesussman

From: **Joseph Land,** landjoseph@charter.net

Subject: **Financial Services Senior Director of Brokerage—Potential Opportunities**

Date: June 2, 2017

To: **Sri Rao,** sri.rao@financerecruiters.com

A winning attitude, cutting-edge industry knowledge, and an expansive, ever-growing network of professional contacts play a key role in my success in the brokerage business. Should you have a client in need of a progressive leader with contagious energy and a drive for sales excellence, you've found him.

Briefly, highlights of my career include:

- **Insurance expert with 25+ years of progressive experience** spanning a broad array of products—life, disability, health, and financial services—in roles that ranged from operations to brokerage sales leadership.

- **Prime driver of a 25%+ surge in premium revenue for a $500 billion industry leader (MassMutual)** by stoking performance from producers in its retail brokerage channel and driving brand awareness.

- **Pioneer of innovative, revenue-generating strategies and tools** that have repeatedly produced high-impact results in best practices, sales analytics, regulatory compliance, and internal audits.

- **Masterful relationship-builder who has an innate ability to attract and influence key players** and forge lasting alliances with agents, general agents, brokers, and industry leaders.

I'd welcome the opportunity to discuss how my expertise can positively impact the growth and success of one of your client's organizations. My resume is attached as a Word document for your review.

Many thanks for your consideration of my qualifications. I look forward to hearing from you soon.

Joseph Land
M: 413.789.9565
landjoseph@charter.net
https://www.linkedin.com/in/landjoseph

The structure of this e-note promotes quick, easy reading. Each bullet points "front-loads" the most meaningful information, using bold type for even greater impact, then follows with just a bit of detail about how and where results were achieved. All of the paragraphs and bullets are short and succinct.

Jill Grindle, CPRW • Pinnacle Resumes, LLC • www.pinnacleresumes.com

From: **Cynthia Evans,** cynthia.evans@gmail.com
Subject: **CFO for Early Stage Companies Seeking Growth—Prior TechStars VP Finance**
Date: April 6, 2017
To: **Robert McCormack,** bob.mccormack@financeheadhunters.net

As Finance VP and CFO, I have been instrumental in building the financial foundation for TechStars and now for Maximize.com. Setting public-company standards *before* the company goes public gives early-stage firms the structure, capability, and credibility they need for rapid and exponential growth.

Just as importantly, I've been involved in creating and maintaining a unique corporate culture that retains and rewards top talent, builds an engaged workforce, and creates exceptional customer satisfaction.

Although secure in my current position, I am confidentially exploring new opportunities with early-stage companies that are seeking their next path to growth. My expertise includes setting strategy, creating processes, building strong teams, and removing obstacles to get projects off the drawing board.

I have had the pleasure of working with extraordinary CEOs, leadership teams, and Boards, and I enjoy a culture of collaboration where I can contribute across many areas of the business.

If one of your clients is seeking a Senior Finance Executive with my expertise, I would welcome your call.

Sincerely,

Cynthia Evans

===================
203-345-6789 • cynthia.evans@gmail.com
LinkedIn.com/in/cynthia-evans

Resume attached

The pedigree for this job seeker—a high-level position with a well-known e-commerce company—is announced immediately, in the subject line and again in the opening sentence. The content of the letter addresses both professional accomplishments and personal preferences for culture and environment.

Louise Kursmark, MRW, CPRW, CCM, JCTC, CEIP • Best Impression Career Services • www.louisekursmark.com

JANE MURRAY

LLM / JD / MBA / CCEP

San Jose, CA 90081 ▪ 412-990-5663 ▪ janemurray@gmail.com

June 5, 2017

Lawrence Torrin, President
McPherson Enterprises
344 Fourth Street
San Jose, CA 90078

Dear Mr. Torrin:

Are you conducting a search for a client company seeking a Chief Compliance Officer who will deliver strategies that move the company forward rather than hinder the business?

As a compliance leader, attorney, and proven commodity, I have successfully administered compliance and legal functions for complex Fortune 500 companies. For these companies, I:

- ✓ **Built two compliance functions recognized as valuable contributors to continued company development and growth.** I set the strategy, vision, mission, and goals; hired staff; and developed the infrastructure, technology, policies, training, and audit tools and processes.

- ✓ **Pinpointed weaknesses and opportunities in the business and drove readiness efforts.** Within the first few years of compliance program inception, we achieved our goals as a compliant federal contractor; all government audits have consistently closed with no findings or fines.

Briefly, my qualifications include:

- ✓ **Legal and compliance experience,** including 11 years at the senior-management level in the startup and management of company-wide compliance and ethics departments.

- ✓ **In-depth knowledge of relevant laws and regulations.** If I don't have the answer, I know how to find it and have an extensive contact base from which to draw expertise.

- ✓ **LLM, JD,** and **MBA** degrees, as well as the **Certified Compliance and Ethics Professional** designation.

A compliance leader who understands the big picture, I am known as a team member who assists business leaders to more appropriately run their businesses—accomplishing goals in a compliant manner. I would welcome a conversation to discuss how my qualifications can benefit your client companies.

Sincerely,

Jane Murray

The dual sets of bullet points, introduced with bold type, make this general-inquiry recruiter letter extremely easy to skim and to read. The opening paragraph immediately communicates a message of value, supported by specific examples of success.

Louise Garver, CERM, CPRW, CJSS, CPBS • Career Directions, LLC • careerdirectionsllc.com

From: **Veronica Santos,** vmsantos@mac.com
Subject: **Sr. Hospitality Executive—International, Profit-Focused, Performance-Driven**
Date: April 2, 2017
To: **Cory Helms,** cory.helms@hospitalityrecruiters.com

In hotel leadership roles spanning the globe, I have tackled unusual challenges and delivered exceptional results:

- **51% EBITDA growth** in 1 year while simultaneously managing 3 Prime Hotels in Argentina. (2016)
- **40% surge in revenue** through strategic refocus on corporate events. (2015)
- **203% growth** in the Prime Rewards loyalty program while spearheading expansion in Asia. (2014)
- **23% increase in GOP** through a dual focus on rate increase and cost control. (2013)

At the corporate level, I have been extensively involved in hotel development, acquisitions, takeovers, and sales. Recently I orchestrated the sale of one of our South American properties at **14X EBITDA.**

In addition, I have a deep understanding of how to build guest-focused operations, engaged teams, and profitable businesses in the luxury niche.

My expertise is improving operations in any area that does not meet the highest expectations—whether that requires attention to guest services, operating efficiencies, new revenue, or a total turnaround. Having worked in 14 cities on 3 continents, I have a multicultural mindset and the ability to get the most from my teams.

If one of your client companies seeks an executive with my track record, I would welcome the opportunity to speak with you. I am open to relocation just about anywhere in the world and will be happy to discuss my compensation requirements during our conversation.

Sincerely,

Veronica Santos
====================
vmsantos@mac.com
+54 25 3456 7890
Skype: veronicamsantos
LinkedIn: linkedin.com/in/veronicamsantos

Starting with the subject line, this e-note delivers a consistent message of achievement and value. The focal point is the 4 bullet points that share specific recent results. Note the reference to "your client companies" in the closing paragraph of this recruiter letter, along with details about relocation and compensation.

Louise Kursmark, MRW, CPRW, CCM, JCTC, CEIP • Best Impression Career Services • www.louisekursmark.com

FELICIA PERRY

Lead by building collaboration, questioning the obvious, encouraging evolution, and rewarding innovation

Mobile 216.702.0094   felicia.perry@gmail.com

May 23, 2017

Brandon Stackpole
Stackpole & Associates
47 Franklin Street
Boston, MA 02212

RE: **Senior Executive Opportunities for President, CEO, COO, EVP, Managing Director, Interim Executive**
     Chemicals, Pharmaceuticals, Engineered Products, Adhesives, Coatings, Polymers, Textiles, Auto Aftermarket

Dear Mr. Stackpole:

In leadership roles driving growth, turnaround, or global expansion for start-ups to Fortune 500 companies, I have consistently delivered double- and triple-digit revenue gains, as highlighted by these examples:

- **Grew operating income 89% on only 10% revenue growth** for Paxton, Inc.
- **Increased EBITDA from $25M to $60M** for ScanSystems International.
- **Spurred 35% revenue gains and tripled operating income** for Acme's Industrial Specialties Division.
- **Identified $50M+ in financial benefits**—new revenue streams, improved cash flow, cost reduction—for Acme Corporate.

Those achievements are indicative of the quality and caliber of my entire professional career. I identify and capitalize on new opportunities, eliminate obstacles, drive product and performance innovation, and orchestrate complex organizational change. My teams and I have delivered unprecedented revenue and earnings growth, outpaced the competition, dominated key industrial and consumer markets, and consistently exceeded investor expectations.

My executive leadership portfolio is complete with a wealth of experience in strategic planning, business/economic/financial analysis, P&L management, operations, multi-channel sales, CRM, marketing, business development, product development, HR, OD, IT, corporate administration, risk management, environmental and regulatory affairs, and corporate facilities.

If you are working with a client company seeking a candidate with my depth of experience and qualifications, I would welcome the chance to speak with you. My recent total compensation package has averaged $300,000+, but money is not the #1 driver. Although I want to be compensated appropriately, I am just as interested in an intriguing opportunity with a significant equity or stock opportunity. In addition, I will relocate for the right opportunity.

I look forward to a conversation.

Sincerely,

Felicia Perry

From the branding statement in the heading through the opening paragraph and 4 strong bullet points, this letter conveys a continuous message of achievement and breadth of experience. The third paragraph is flush with relevant keywords, and the fourth paragraph shares additional recruiter-appropriate information.

Wendy Enelow, MRW, CCM, JCTC, CPRW • Enelow Executive Career Services • www.wendyenelow.com

CHAPTER 5:
Networking Letters

What Is a Networking Letter?

Networking is the single most effective way to find a new position. When you network into a company, you immediately distance yourself from every other candidate who has written a job posting or cold call letter. You've become an insider, and that gives you a tremendous advantage in landing a new position.

To make the magic of networking work for you, you'll need to write **strong networking letters that will help your network contacts help you.** Read on to learn how to do that.

> **Pro Tip: A networking letter makes a connection between you and someone you know.** That someone could be anyone ... an acquaintance, a colleague or former manager, an executive from outside your company, a neighbor, a family member, someone you worship with or volunteer with, or a fellow member of a professional association.
>
> The possibilities are endless, and the only requirement is for that person to know who you are. Your letter will provide all the details to make it easy for that contact to help you.

What Do You Want to Achieve in Your Networking Letter?

You have 3 primary goals in writing a networking letter:

- Let your network contact know *specifically* how she can help you.
- Get names and contact information of people whom your network contact knows.
- Begin a dialogue with your contact and set the stage for further conversations.

Not every letter will address all 3 of these goals, but never lose sight of the fact that your initial networking outreach is just the beginning of the conversation.

Goal #1: Help Your Contacts Help You

In your networking letter, share information that gives your contacts a framework for helping you, referring you, and describing you to others. Keep in mind that you are reaching out to people you know—people who like you and are inclined to support you. Make it easy for them!

Key points to share with your network include the following:

- **Who you are—your current career focus.** While, presumably, your contacts know a good deal about you, it is helpful to *them* if you give them precise language and relevant details. And it's helpful to *you* if you position yourself for your current goals—rather than relying on contacts who might know you from a past position or even a prior career.

- **What you know and what you have achieved.** Again, your contacts may not know your latest and greatest achievements or your current level of expertise. Share a few highlights that will help them understand your value and be able to convey that value to others.

- **Specifically how they can help.** When you ask vaguely for "help" without further details, your contacts may be at a loss. Be sure to ask for what you want. Do you need an introduction to a certain company? Insider knowledge about an industry development? Advice and insight regarding your job search?

Goal #2: Expand Your Network

We refer to people you know—your direct network—as Tier 1 contacts. What you want from them are Tier 2 contacts—the people they know. And what you want from Tier 2 are Tier 3 contacts. Just think … If you have a network of 40 people, with just 3 contacts from each you can triple your network to 120, and then triple it again to 360. That's a lot of people who will get to know who you are and the value you offer.

Of course, not every one of your Tier 1 and Tier 2 contacts will give you 3 names, but even if you get only 50% of the 360 total, you are well on your way to reaching a decision maker, finding a great opportunity, and landing a new job.

More often than not, the real interviewing action will come from your Tier 2 and Tier 3 connections. If people in your direct Tier 1 network are hiring or know of a specific job, they'll let you know. No need to ask and get "no" for an answer. Instead, ask for something they can easily give you—a contact or referral.

Many of your network contacts will offer to make an introduction on your behalf via phone or email. If so, great! That instantly expands your network and makes for a "warm" connection instead of a "cold call."

At a minimum, ask your contacts if you can mention their names when you reach out to the people they suggest. These letters—referral letters—are addressed in Chapter 6.

Goal #3: Start a Dialogue

Most of the networking letters you will read in this chapter request a meeting or phone call. That's a good tactic to keep the conversation going, and it usually requires that you reach out to schedule that meeting.

As we've stated before, it's to your advantage to keep the ball in your court—simply because your job search is of *primary* importance to you and much less important to others. Most of your contacts will be willing to help and will be even happier if you take the initiative to follow up.

How Do You Write a Networking Letter?

How you write a networking letter depends entirely on your relationship with each person to whom you're writing.

In almost all instances, your networking letters will include information similar to what you include in all of your job search letters—highlights of your achievements, work experience, educational credentials, and other distinguishing information. However, the tone, style, and familiarity of every networking letter will differ with each recipient.

> **Pro Tip: If you haven't been in touch with someone for years, do a LinkedIn or Google search to find information that you can use in the introduction.** Not only is the Internet a great way for you to reach out to others, it is just as valuable as a research tool.

Consider these different scenarios to decide the best approach to take in reaching out to your networking contacts—from a very casual quick note to a professional letter.

- **When writing to a very close friend or family member** who knows a great deal about your career, a simple e-note summarizing a few highlights, along with a statement about your career objectives, is plenty to share. You might think that these close contacts don't need a letter, but they'll find it helpful to have specific information at their fingertips.

- **When writing to neighbors, casual acquaintances, members of organizations that you belong to or volunteer with, or other people you know, but not well,** write a more complete letter, similar to what you'd write for a cold call letter. What will differ greatly is the introductory paragraph. You'll want to immediately establish the connection and remind them how or why they know you.

- **If you have been out of college or vocational school for a good number of years and are writing letters to reconnect** with college friends and roommates, you'll need to catch them up with what you've been doing and clearly establish your current professional persona. Before launching into your letter content, be sure to start with a friendly reconnection.

- **If you are writing to a professional colleague,** your introduction will vary based on how well you know that particular individual. If it is someone you have worked with every day for the past 5 years, the introduction can be casual. But be careful if it is a current colleague—you do not want to jeopardize your current position at the same company!

  If it is a colleague you worked with in the past, first reconnect, and then explain why you are writing.

- **When writing to a past supervisor, manager, or company executive,** you will want to be more formal in your introductory paragraph. How you address that person—by first name or Mr./Ms. last name—depends on your relationship. Customize your introduction as appropriate. Someone you worked with a year ago will know who you are, but if it has been years and years, you might need to jog her memory.

How Do You Submit a Networking Letter?

A 2-pronged approach may get you the best results when using a networking letter.

Step One

Whenever possible and appropriate, take a few minutes to make a phone call to let your contact know that you are in the market for a new position and would like to send a letter and resume so he can make some recommendations and share a few contacts.

The phone call is a friendly and personal way to launch your networking campaign, depending on your relationship with that individual and how comfortable you are making that call. It is much easier to call your brother-in-law than a top executive at a company you worked at 5 years ago.

Nonetheless, we recommend that you make the call whenever possible, even if it is a bit uncomfortable. Once you have made the phone connection, the person will be aware that your email is coming and, hopefully, be willing to help.

In the rare instances when contacts tell you that they cannot help you, that is fine. Just thank them for their time, wish them the best, and encourage them to reach out to you if there is ever anything you can do for them. Remember, networking is a 2-way street. And, you never know ... simply by sharing your latest career quest with your contacts, you become top of mind with them. If they hear something that would be helpful or relevant to you, they will often get in touch.

Step Two

To transmit your networking letter and resume, we recommend email 99% of the time. It is quick and efficient, and it allows your network contact to easily pass your information along to others.

As always, use the content of your networking letter as your email message so you can instantly engage your reader. There's no need to attach the letter as a separate file.

Should you include a resume when you are sending a networking letter? In our opinion, a resounding yes! The whole point of networking is to continually increase the number of people who know about you, your career, your credentials, and all that you have accomplished. Your network contacts may know you well, but it is still advisable to send your resume so they will know all of the specifics and can share with others.

The only situations when you might not want to send your resume with your networking letter are:

- When a network contact is a bit tentative in responding to your initial phone call. In that instance, your networking letter is a good place to start without applying too much pressure.

- When it just doesn't feel right or seems a bit too assertive. When in doubt, trust your instincts, and just email the letter.

Who Is the Audience?

The audience for networking letters is just about every single person that you know—professionally and personally. Here is a list of ideas to help you get started in building your network and accelerating your job search:

- Professional Colleagues
- Employees Who Worked For You
- Supervisors & Managers
- Company Executives
- Fellow Association Members
- Fellow Church Members
- Fellow Volunteers
- Casual Acquaintances
- Family Members
- Friends & Neighbors

Of course, you'll want to maintain the appropriate level of confidentiality based on your specific situation. If you're currently employed, you will not want to share details of your search with certain people, so don't include them in your network. But if you're not currently working and are actively job searching, reach out to everyone.

> **Pro Tip: When building your network, never discount anyone because you never know who others know!** That is the intrinsic value of networking letters: You can go far beyond your own personal network, tap into the networks of others, multiply your reach, and accelerate your job search.

To Whom Do You Send It?

As just discussed, send your letter to each contact you can find—people you know now and others with whom you want to rekindle a relationship.

What are the Unique Characteristics of a Networking Letter?

To understand the nuances of each of the networking letters on the next 10 pages, be certain to read the box at the bottom of every letter. You'll find specifics about each letter—why it was written the way that it was, the most important elements of that letter, and other important insights.

From: **George P. Burdell IV,** gpburdell4@yahoo.com
Subject: **Georgia Tech Career Fair Follow-up**
Date: March 23, 2017
To: **Dan Kennedy,** danielkennedy@kbr.com

Mr. Kennedy, I enjoyed meeting you at the Georgia Tech Career Fair last week and am following up regarding a career in the engineering and construction industry.

I will be graduating in a few months with a BS in Electrical Engineering and looking to start my career. After our meeting and some additional research into KBR, I've placed your company at the top of my list!

Several reasons I believe I would be a great candidate to join your team:

➢ For the last 3 years I co-op'ed with Bechtel, one of the leading EPCM companies in the world. I gained a lot of real-world engineering experience and consistently received "outstanding" evaluations.

➢ I focused my studies in the areas of Power Engineering and Systems and Controls (critical to what KBR does so well) as well as Leadership and Entrepreneurship.

➢ I was chosen as a member of the FASET Orientation Board, one of the most highly selective positions for undergraduates at Georgia Tech.

Even if KBR does not have any upcoming openings that would be suitable for me, I would still like the opportunity to meet with you to learn more about your career—how you got where you are today—and get your advice for my next professional steps.

I look forward to talking with you in the near future and will call your office to schedule a time. Thank you.

Sincerely,

George P. Burdell, IV
Atlanta, Georgia
(404) 889-2536
gpburdell4@yahoo.com

Resume attached

Following up a brief or casual meeting is a great approach for a networking letter. This e-note for a soon-to-graduate engineer goes on to cite experiences that should be valuable to the company he's targeting. Notice that he asks for a meeting even if no specific opportunities exist.

Sharon M. Bowden, CPRW, CEIP • SMB Solutions • www.startsavvy.com

From:	**Rachael Malkov,** rachael.malkov@emerson.edu
Subject:	**Your latest Forbes article blew me away!**
Date:	January 23, 2017
To:	**Alyse Standish,** akstandish@dataanalysts.com

Hi Alyse,

You might recall we met briefly at the Analytics Innovation event last fall. Since then I've been following your work at Etsy, and the insights you shared in your Forbes article are amazing!

I would like to learn more about your path in business intelligence. My next career step is a role in marketing, and hearing about your experiences as an Analytics Specialist would help orient my thinking in a powerful way.

Would you consider letting me buy you a coffee near your office next week?

Looking forward,

Rachael Malkov

Rachael Malkov
Research Associate, Emerson College
www.linkedin/in/malkov
315-782-7975

Networking letters often are less formal than traditional cover letters—even when the connection is not especially strong, as in this e-note. The brevity, directness, and breeziness of this message make it fresh, inviting, and difficult to resist.

Erica Breuer, CPS • Cake Resumes • www.cakeresumes.com

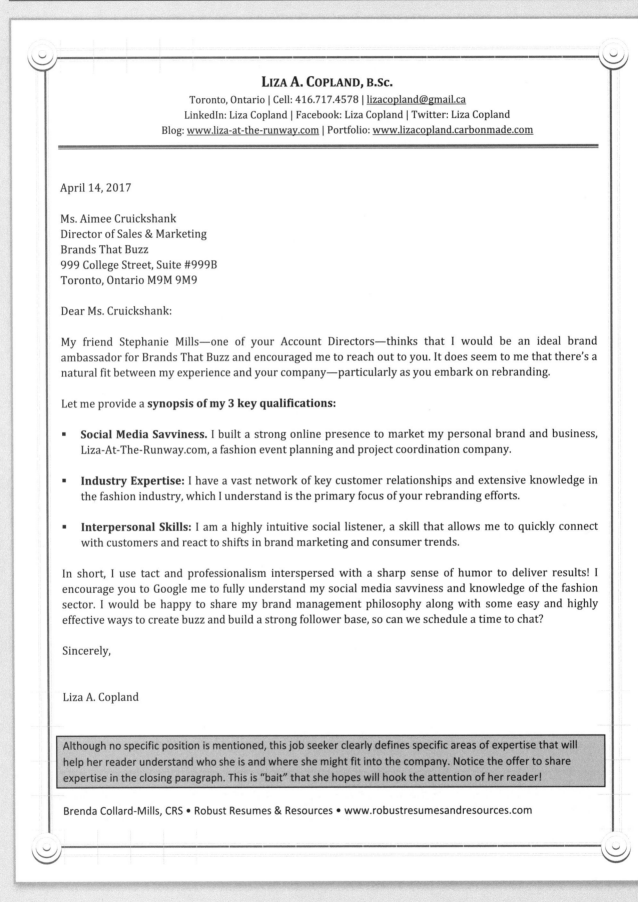

LIZA A. COPLAND, B.Sc.

Toronto, Ontario | Cell: 416.717.4578 | lizacopland@gmail.ca
LinkedIn: Liza Copland | Facebook: Liza Copland | Twitter: Liza Copland
Blog: www.liza-at-the-runway.com | Portfolio: www.lizacopland.carbonmade.com

April 14, 2017

Ms. Aimee Cruickshank
Director of Sales & Marketing
Brands That Buzz
999 College Street, Suite #999B
Toronto, Ontario M9M 9M9

Dear Ms. Cruickshank:

My friend Stephanie Mills—one of your Account Directors—thinks that I would be an ideal brand ambassador for Brands That Buzz and encouraged me to reach out to you. It does seem to me that there's a natural fit between my experience and your company—particularly as you embark on rebranding.

Let me provide a **synopsis of my 3 key qualifications:**

- **Social Media Savviness.** I built a strong online presence to market my personal brand and business, Liza-At-The-Runway.com, a fashion event planning and project coordination company.

- **Industry Expertise:** I have a vast network of key customer relationships and extensive knowledge in the fashion industry, which I understand is the primary focus of your rebranding efforts.

- **Interpersonal Skills:** I am a highly intuitive social listener, a skill that allows me to quickly connect with customers and react to shifts in brand marketing and consumer trends.

In short, I use tact and professionalism interspersed with a sharp sense of humor to deliver results! I encourage you to Google me to fully understand my social media savviness and knowledge of the fashion sector. I would be happy to share my brand management philosophy along with some easy and highly effective ways to create buzz and build a strong follower base, so can we schedule a time to chat?

Sincerely,

Liza A. Copland

Although no specific position is mentioned, this job seeker clearly defines specific areas of expertise that will help her reader understand who she is and where she might fit into the company. Notice the offer to share expertise in the closing paragraph. This is "bait" that she hopes will hook the attention of her reader!

Brenda Collard-Mills, CRS • Robust Resumes & Resources • www.robustresumesandresources.com

From: **Nicole Bradley,** nicole_bradley@email.com
Subject: **Connecting you with career "karma"**
Date: April 24, 2017
To: **Mark Boudreau,** mark.boudreau@digitalmarketing.com

Hi Mark,

We're connected on LinkedIn and I noticed that you recently viewed my profile. This is a happy coincidence because I just applied for an Account Manager role at your advertising agency.

I really admire what you and your team are doing in the digital marketing space. Specifically, I love the creative campaign for Aqua Blast Water that I am currently seeing everywhere.

My experience includes account management, program implementation, and creative problem solving. I worked with clients such as Unilever, Procter & Gamble, and PepsiCo—both directly and with international agencies servicing those companies.

With the hopes of creating a little career "karma" that will give my job hunt a boost, I'm wondering if you could spare 20 minutes for a coffee or phone chat. I'd love to learn more about your career history and the work you are most "fired up" about these days.

How about Wednesday at 11:30, or I'm available anytime on Friday …

Connecting with you on LinkedIn is fine, but I'm looking forward to connecting with you in person!

Warmly,

Nicole Bradley
nicole_bradley@email.com
416-825-9834
www.linkedin.com/in/nicolejbradley

"Connecting on LinkedIn is fine," but an in-person connection is so much more valuable—and this e-note is a great example of how to move an online connection to the next level. This job seeker is making excellent use of the LinkedIn feature that allows users to see who is viewing their profile.

Beth Yarzab • CareerFit Mom • www.careerfitmom.ca

Stephan Weber

www.linkedin.com/in/stephanweber

312-625-9756
info@weber.com

TECHNOLOGY SALES CONSULTANT
Enterprise Content Management Systems ▪ Document Management

June 30, 2017

John Walter
Dropbox Inc.
333 Brannan Street
San Francisco, CA 94107

Dear Mr. Walter:

In our recent conversation on LinkedIn, I expressed my interest in exploring career opportunities with Dropbox. My expertise is acting as the liaison between external customers and internal technology teams to move sales projects forward, deliver product solutions, and help customers simplify their business processes.

And, as an avid Dropbox user myself, I can visualize, strategize, plan, and deliver solutions to help customers make the most of the features and functionality of your technology solutions. My experience includes:

- **Technology.** For the past 9 years, I have directed international projects in process design and implementation of IT solutions, ECM Systems, CRM, Project Management, Print Management Concepts and Office Communication Systems, selling products, services, software, and hardware to clients worldwide.

- **Customer Relationship Management & User Support.** Managing relationships with customers worldwide and providing oversight of global user support operations, I understand how to communicate with clients, identify their needs, solve problems, deliver timely solutions, and build strong relationships.

- **Communication.** Throughout my career, I have been repeatedly commended for my exceptionally strong cross-cultural communication skills with everyone from end users to senior management executives.

- **Sales Affairs.** I have worked with Fortune 500 corporations and international clients to develop and deliver solutions to our global technology and infrastructure development needs.

At ECM Systems, I was recognized as a top performer with excellent customer satisfaction scores and achieved the highest sales objectives for a software developer, being awarded "Best Employee" in 2015.

As I seek to strengthen my skills as a sales professional within the technology industry, I look forward to gaining your insight into how I might bring my value to Dropbox. What would be a good time for me to call?

Sincerely,

Stephan Weber

enclosure: resume

After initiating a conversation on LinkedIn, the job seeker seeks to move the discussion offline through a letter that details his expertise, his value, and—very importantly—his knowledge of the company and its products. Every paragraph and bullet is filled with relevant information, yet written succinctly for an easy read.

Maike Hennig, ACRW • www.maikehennig.com

DOUG SHULTZ

Auditor ▪ Investigator ▪ Leader

303.788.2142
dshultz@gmail.com
Denver Metro

March 6, 2017

Ms. Kelly Reed
Central Intelligence Agency
Human Resources
Box 27, Department HR52
Washington, DC 20505

Dear Ms. Reed:

Tom Burton told me about your field auditor challenges and recommended that we meet. While I understand that you may not have an auditor job opening at this time, we share mutual aspirations and I can provide you with helpful resources. Likewise, I would like to learn more about your team challenges and the Central Intelligence Agency.

Auditing is my passion! Throughout my career, my high standards and commitment to excellence have generated recommendations that strengthened internal controls and processes. I excel at connecting with people, documenting findings, communicating solutions, and identifying opportunities that reduce risks. Currently, I'm researching organizations to understand internal cultures and operating practices.

Whether or not we work together in the future, I know a discussion will be beneficial to us both. Are you available to meet on Tuesday, March 21, at 11:00 am? Or is there another time that will work better with your schedule? Please call me at 303.788.2142 to arrange a meeting.

So that you know a bit more about my experience and expertise when we meet, I have attached my resume. Thank you in advance for your time.

Sincerely,

Doug Shultz

This well-written networking letter very explicitly states that "you may not have an auditor job opening at this time" but makes a strong case for why a meeting would be valuable—and goes on to suggest a specific date and time for that meeting in an effort to move this networking connection forward.

Ruth Pankratz, MRW, NCRW, CPRW • Gabby Communications • www.gabbycommunications.com

Bill Pinto

630.555.1234 • Palatine, IL 60067 • billpinto@gmail.com • www.linkedin.com/billpinto

June 1, 2017

Mr. Richard Ruff
Motorola
500 Coventry Lane
Crystal Lake, IL 60014

Dear Richard:

Congratulations on your recent promotion to COO and General Manager for Devices! From what I recall in our Verizon days, I know you are going to do great things in that role.

With the rapidly moving mobile technology environment, especially IoT, I suspect anticipating demands before they emerge will be critical for you to generate new revenue sources.

In my current position as VP of Business Development at Interconnect, we had a similar challenge. Our sales model wasn't scalable, and executive management wasn't sure how to pivot. With the new part of the spectrum becoming available in 2017, I noticed a lot of changes that would benefit our customers. I created a strategy to take advantage of this, and it allowed us to land development projects worth **+$1M with Facebook, the PGA, and Emerson.**

As a former RIM employee who led the distribution model change from customer direct to carrier, I can see how this same spectrum opportunity can benefit Motorola. If you're interested in getting ahead of the curve and being able to implement more secure and reliable networks for your customers, I would love to talk.

Best regards,

Bill Pinto

Enclosure

When a former colleague earns a promotion, this job seeker makes a point to reach out and reconnect. He goes on to share ideas and experiences that may help his colleague be more successful ... and, not incidentally, that might involve hiring him to make those great ideas happen! Notice the impact of his bolded achievement.

Michelle Robin, NCRW, CPRW • Brand Your Career • www.brandyourcareer.com

From: **Trevor Harris,** trevor.harris@mac.com
Subject: **Tech startup research—referred by Sarah Williams**
Date: May 18, 2017
To: **Amy Ryan,** amy_ryan@techstarters.com

Dear Ms. Ryan:

At yesterday's Los Angeles Venture Association forum, I was fortunate to meet Sarah Williams, who suggested I reach out to you for insight into Silicon Beach tech startups.

Having recently relocated to LA, I'm beginning to expand my network within the Silicon Beach community and gather more information on startups here.

From your LinkedIn profile, I see that you have extensive startup experience; I've also been in the industry for many years, most recently as VP of Business Development for a SaaS startup in Silicon Valley.

Throughout my career, I've been passionate about B2B startups with disruptive technology that can transform customers' operations. Based on your work at AnalyticsNOW, I suspect we have a lot in common!

I know I would benefit from your knowledge of Silicon Beach startups, and I'm very interested in learning more about AnalyticsNOW. And, I'll be happy to help you in any way I can, of course. I'm sure you're busy, but I'm hoping you have time for a short chat, so which day this week or next would be most convenient for me to stop by your office briefly?

All the best,

Trevor Harris
415-945-5534
trevor.harris@mac.com
www.linkedin.com/in/techtrevor

In just a few short paragraphs, this e-note communicates "who, what, and why" so that the reader instantly understands the reason for the contact and the potential value to her. The closing is quite assertive—assuming that a meeting will be scheduled—and easy to respond to.

Kelly Donovan, CPRW • Kelly Donovan & Associates • www.kellydonovan.com

From:	**Mark Richards,** mrichards@gmail.com
Subject:	**Reconnecting …**
Date:	May 23, 2017
To:	**Roger Summers,** roger.summers@ge.com.uk

Dear Roger,

It's been some time since we worked together at *GE* and I would like to reconnect. I currently work for *Baker Hughes* in a high-risk area of Iraq, managing a **$349M** client portfolio. With oil & gas prices causing market uncertainty and high security risks, I seek new business development and integrated project management opportunities. ***I ask you to consider sharing my name, skill sets, and accomplishments with your robust network of respected colleagues and friends.***

Customizing turnkey customer solutions is what I do best. As you know, I helped grow our *GE* portfolio from **$200M** to **$1B+**, applying well-researched competitor and customer awareness, due diligence, and client relationship management to close lucrative deals. These successes, along with others at *3M*, *Halliburton*, and *Siemens AG,* resulted in BIG WINS like these:

- ➡ Collecting **$65M** of outstanding payments and cutting DSO from **146** to **65**.
- ➡ Uncovering new opportunities with a 5-year business plan that turned a **<$200M** portfolio into a **$2B** operation.
- ➡ Protecting stakeholders from high-risk contracts—e.g., hedging FX exposure that would have cost *Baker Hughes* **$3M**.

I've always admired your ability to judge situations fairly. I trust your advice and hope we can speak soon to discuss how I may help you or someone in your network looking for a business development leader. Review my resume and let's discuss further. I'll call next week to schedule an appointment.

Best regards,

Mark Richards
(312) 456-5578 ✦ mrichards@gmail.com

Resume attached

This e-note writer is very explicit in his request for help—highlighted in bold at the end of the first paragraph. He includes reminders of achievements from the time he worked with the reader, plus recent accomplishments, and closes with a promise to call. The use of bold for all numbers makes them jump off the page.

Kimberly A. Sernel, CPA, ACRW, CPRW • Horizon Career Solutions • www.horizoncareersolutions.com

AVALYN A. JONES

(914) 560-2786 ✦ aamara@gmail.com
www.linkedin.com/in/avalyna

May 23, 2017

Steven Nichols, Partner
Capital Investment Plus, LLC
222 Crescent Avenue
Chicago, IL 60605

Dear Mr. Nichols:

At the suggestion of **Steven Adler**, my good friend and Board of Directors' colleague at *Greco Funds*, I'm reaching out to request an introductory meeting. Steven believes I bring a diverse and valuable perspective to board leadership and thought you would be interested in my background.

With 20+ years of F500 management, academia, and board leadership, I promote strong governance and board engagement. To encourage healthy debate, I ask tough questions and bring fresh perspectives. Highlights:

✓ *Greco Funds, Non-Executive Chair:* Our Board overhauled the portfolio with a 5-year strategic plan. We required a 6%+ minimum annual distribution and rebranded and marketed the fund's rich history.

✓ *AIG, Board Director:* Overcoming regulatory concerns, we replaced management and oversaw 2 major M&As that put the operation into a #1 market position.

✓ *State Farm, Board Director:* In 3 years, we created industry-respected governance and risk management practices, turning **$21M** losses into **$80M** gains.

> **VALUE PURSUED & DELIVERED**
> ✓ Heightened emphasis on corporate governance and professionalism.
> ✓ Taught executives as a Finance Professor at Yale, Stanford, and INSEAD.
> ✓ Consulted with leaders in international accounting standards and equity markets.
> ✓ Built consensus among competing voices, respecting diversity and Board independence.

I believe in highly engaged boards acting as evangelists for the company's interests. I am currently targeting boards looking for a **Chair** or **Member** who brings big ideas, knows what risks to take, and oversees execution. I would appreciate your insight into my search and will call next week to schedule an appointment. Thank you.

Best regards,

Avalyn A. Jones

Enclosure: Resume

Opening with a strong referral, this networking letter clearly establishes the reason for getting in touch—a board appointment. The shaded box highlighting "Value" balances 3 strong bullet points of specific board-level achievements. Using an assertive close, the final paragraph requests a meeting to gain further insight.

Kimberly A. Sernel, CPA, ACRW, CPRW • Horizon Career Solutions • www.horizoncareersolutions.com

CHAPTER 6:
Referral Letters

What Is a Referral Letter?

A referral letter is one of the most effective tools that you can have in your job search portfolio. Why? Because you are sending it at the suggestion or recommendation of someone else—one of your contacts who knows the person to whom you are sending the letter. That referral will often open the door to a conversation and, hopefully, an interview.

Here's an example. You know Robert from when you worked at General Electric. Robert happens to be good friends with someone who works at Hewlett Packard, a company that you are quite interested in. Robert shares Emily's contact info at HP and you write a letter to Emily. Emily is happy to connect with someone referred to her by Robert … so you're in the door.

> **Pro Tip: You are virtually guaranteed to get an interview if you are referred for an available position,** provided you have the requisite qualifications for the job. Yes, *guaranteed!* According to extensive research done over the years by our colleague Gerry Crispin at CareerXRoads, referred candidates will be interviewed **100%** of the time if they are qualified.
>
> When you understand the odds in your favor, we think you'll be extremely motivated to reach out to your network and get referred to their contacts.

Referral letters can be considered extensions of networking letters because they have many of the same characteristics. In fact, leveraging referrals *is* a type of networking. The one thing that distinguishes referral letters is what you write at the very beginning of each letter—the referral that prompted you to get in touch. We will discuss how to write these letters in more detail further in this chapter.

> **Pro Tip: Referral letters are *not* reference letters.** In a referral letter you introduce yourself to someone who was recommended to you by an individual you both know. A reference letter, in contrast, is a letter written by someone else attesting to the quality of your work.

What Do You Want to Achieve in Your Referral Letter?

You should have 2 distinct goals in mind when writing your referral letter. First, you want to make an instant connection with the reader by sharing the name of the person who referred you. Rather than approaching someone as a total stranger, you now share a connection. Your letter is not a cold call but rather a warm outreach.

Your second objective is the same as with most job search letters—an interview or, at the very least, a phone conversation to learn more about the company and its current hiring needs. Because you have been referred, you are very likely to get the chance for a conversation. Even if it's just a quick phone call, use those few minutes wisely. Ask about that person's company and potential hiring needs, but also inquire about other individuals to whom they can refer you or other companies that might be interested in a candidate with your qualifications.

How Do You Write a Referral Letter?

The single most important consideration when writing a referral letter is to include the name of the person who referred you in both the subject line and the very first sentence—if possible, at the beginning of the first sentence.

Mentioning your referral source creates an instant connection between yourself and the person you have contacted. You are not simply a stranger. You are someone who is already in the circle of that person's personal or professional network. It makes a huge difference in the initial reaction and response to your letter.

> **Pro Tip: Explain the connection if necessary.** At times you may be referred to a person who doesn't know the referral source very well. Your introduction will lose its power if that person's name is not instantly familiar to your new contact.
>
> An example might be when a friend who works at one of your target companies tells you the name of the hiring manager for a particular job but doesn't know that hiring manager personally. In that case, mention the connection instantly in your opening sentence: *"Abby Carmichael, your field sales manager in Dubuque, suggested I contact you regarding your current need for a Graphic Designer."*

Carefully read all of the sample letters in this chapter and you will get plenty of ideas for how to start your referral letters. The first sentence can make or break you. The connection must be immediate and, as with all of your job search letters, the content must be strong.

The remaining content of your referral letters will be similar to other job search letters you write. Focus on the skills, experiences, achievements, educational and professional credentials, and other qualifications that you believe will be of most value to each individual and company you are contacting.

The letter does not have to be exceptionally long, but it does need to impress your reader. Do not simply state your skills. Instead, highlight how you have used those skills to positively impact your employer(s).

How Do You Submit a Referral Letter?

You will use referral letters much like you use networking letters—to reach out to individual contacts as an effective way to identify and explore new career opportunities.

Just as with other letters, send this as an e-note—the letter right in the body of the email message so it is quick and easy to read. Your referral's name, along with the content of your letter, should make an instant impression on the reader and create the opportunity for an interview. Attach your resume as a PDF (preferred) or Word file.

If your contact has given you the phone number for the referral, we strongly recommend that you call before you send your letter. A call is a powerful and personal way to start building the relationship and to let this individual know to be on the lookout for your letter and resume.

Who Is the Audience?

The specific audience for referral letters can vary widely. It depends entirely on the referrals that you gain from your network contacts. Just as with networking letters, referral letters can be written to:

- Professional Colleagues
- Past Co-Workers
- Supervisors & Managers
- Company Executives
- Fellow Association Members
- Fellow Church Members
- Fellow Volunteers
- Casual Acquaintances
- Family Members
- Friends & Neighbors

Referral letters are extremely effective in expanding your network of contacts and in generating interviews. We recommend that you make them a central pillar of your job search campaign.

To Whom Do You Send It?

It's simple and straightforward: Send a referral letter to anyone and everyone whose name and contact information you can glean from your own network.

What Are the Unique Characteristics of a Referral Letter?

On the following pages, you will find 10 sample referral letters. Take the time to review the many different styles of letters, pay attention to the variety in tone and content, and use them as models for your own letters. The box at the bottom of each page provides specific notes and insights for that particular letter.

From:	**Matt Bradley,** mattfbradley@mac.com
Subject:	**Director of Sponsorships—Referred by DIANA SMITH**
Date:	May 13, 2017
To:	**Gerhardt Gecht,** ggecht@impactsolutions.com

Dr. Gecht—

Diana Smith suggested I contact you in regards to the Events Manager position with IMPACT Solutions. Collaborating together on the 2016 Nashville Wellness Convention, Diana has witnessed firsthand my:

Connections to association and community leaders throughout Northern Tennessee.
→ Secured the Mayor as Master of Ceremonies, drawing record-breaking crowds.

Ability to drive results and cultivate strong relationships.
→ Accelerated revenue with $23K+ in new corporate sponsorships.

Skill for empowering individuals and teams to drive toward a shared vision.
→ Managed more than 350 volunteers over 4-day event.

The attached resume illustrates many of my accomplishments—measurable projects that demonstrate the type of bottom-line value I can bring to IMPACT Solutions.

I welcome the opportunity to meet with you to discuss your department's needs and how I might make a positive IMPACT as a key member of your team. I will call you next week to schedule a conversation.

Sincerely,

Matt F. Bradley
****

540-731-0889
mattfbradley@mac.com
www.linkedin.com/in/mattbradley
www.about.me/mattbradley

After mentioning the name of the person who referred him (twice—once in the subject line and again in the opening sentence), this e-note goes on to cite 3 specific, relevant skills paired with 3 measurable achievements. The letter is crisp, tightly written, and perfectly customized to this opportunity at this organization.

Kris McGuigan, ACRW, CCMC • Professional Courage LLC • professionalcourage.com

From:	**Kwame Jackson,** kwame@kwamejackson.com
Subject:	**MLB–Los Angeles Stars Staff Writer Opening (Referral by Joan Franklin)**
Date:	June 24, 2017
To:	**Willie Greene,** williegreen@phpmedia.com

Mr. Greene,

Joan Franklin advised that you currently have an opening for a full-time staff writer covering the Los Angeles Stars. I appreciate having a few minutes of your time to introduce myself for this position.

I come "Star ready." I am familiar with the team's history, players, coaches, and front office personnel. This knowledge has added depth to my writing over my 15-year career and has taught me the value of building collaborative relationships both within the franchise and around the league.

I also offer intangibles that will help me promote and build PHP Media's audience:

➤ **A strong social media presence.** I have 12.2K+ Twitter followers with whom I interact daily, discussing the Stars as well as other significant league-wide issues. I am also proficient in using advanced social media tools to strategically promote my content at high-peak periods throughout the day. This approach has led to both a steady increase in followers and an even greater gain in article page views.

➤ **Creativity and innovation.** I recognize the challenges of the Los Angeles sports media market and the need to be innovative, creative, and readable. Through research, an eye on the competition, and an awareness of what my readers want, I consistently find unique angles that generate page views and reader loyalty.

➤ **Networks and resources.** I have maintained long-term relationships with numerous league personnel, managed a steady schedule of in-person and social media engagements, and built a sizeable network of resources to add extra dimension to my reporting on a year-round basis

In addition to being a storyteller, I have, over the last year, created, produced, co-hosted, and distributed (via iTunes) a very successful podcast, "Stars Gazing," which has been downloaded 3M+ times as of this writing.

I hope these credentials as well as those outlined on my resume (attached as a PDF) and my clip portfolio (linked below) have convinced you that a meeting to discuss PHP Media's Los Angeles Stars staff writer position would be beneficial. I will call in a few days to schedule a convenient time. Thank you!

Kwame Jackson
****
kwame@kwamejackson.com • 908-873-2240
Los Angeles Stars Beat Writer—Worldwide Sports Media Inc.
Select Clip Library: http://www.kwamejackson.com/portfolio

A bit longer than many e-notes, this letter is chock-full of information that is highly relevant to the specific and very competitive position. Notice the many references to the local team (the Stars), the local market (Los Angeles), and valuable social media skills and experience (with measurable results).

From: Jane Consuelos, janeconsuelos@yahoo.com
Subject: Project Manager Resource
Date: June 3, 2017
To: Alex Hutchinson, a.hutchinson@trebuchet.com

Dear Mr. Hutchinson:

Lee Marshall told me about Trebuchet Engineering, and after researching your firm, I'm impressed! I was delighted to see your project manager position listed on the CSU alumni career website.

For the past year, I have been assisting the Rawhide Energy team. We've implemented a new system at our facility that reduces energy consumption by replacing dilapidated equipment. Overseeing complex projects like this is my passion. Additional career specialties of mine include:

- Planning and scheduling resources to achieve project goals.
- Communicating daily with clients and senior managers regarding project progress.
- Negotiating with contractors and suppliers for materials and services.

My education, work experience, and skills are a few reasons why I would be an excellent addition to Trebuchet Engineering.

After you review my attached resume, please contact me. I will make myself available for a meeting at your convenience.

Sincerely,

Jane Consuelos
▪▪▪▪▪▪▪▪▪▪▪▪▪▪▪▪▪▪▪▪▪▪▪▪

970.366.8259
janeconsuelos@yahoo.com
LinkedIn.com/in/janeconsuelos

This e-note conveys enthusiasm and energy—powerful yet intangible qualities that the job seeker brings to every employer and every project. A highlight of the letter is an anecdote about a recent team project, followed by 3 bullet points that convey additional skills.

Ruth Pankratz, MRW, NCRW, CPRW • Gabby Communications • www.gabbycommunications.com

SHARON DERBY

Providence, RI | (436) 569-4862 | sderby@email.com

April 29, 2017

Fred Lippon
Office Manager
South Providence Dermatology
Cranston, RI 02910

Dear Mr. Lippon:

A few weeks ago I met Dr. Leone and spoke with her about my experience as a Nurse Practitioner. She encouraged me to reach out to you to express my interest in joining South Providence Dermatology. I am excited about exploring a position with your practice and believe that I have the required skill set and relevant experience to excel. I can offer:

- **Exceptional, individualized patient care, including assessment, treatment, and ongoing patient education,** as demonstrated by my experience working with 10–15 patients a day at Plainfield Walk-In Medical Clinic, Mineral Spring Primary Care, and Memorial Hospital of Rhode Island.

- **Current nursing qualifications,** including Rhode Island Nursing License, Rhode Island State Nurse Practitioner License, Master of Science in Nursing, and membership in the American Academy of Nurse Practitioners.

- **Analytical, problem-solving mindset and attention to detail,** utilized throughout my nursing career. Working under fast-paced conditions, I have multi-tasked to manage the changing needs of various patient caseloads.

I pride myself on my ability to follow through with my work, and I am able to learn new clinical skills with ease.

I have heard nothing but wonderful things about your group and would be delighted to join your team! I look forward to speaking with you and will phone your office next week to schedule a meeting.

Sincerely,

Sharon Derby, MSN, APRN, ANP-C

To overcome lack of experience in the specific field of dermatology, this job seeker emphasizes relevant skills and experience that will make her a success in any area of nursing. She further mentions that she is "able to learn new clinical skills with ease." The closing paragraph again touches on the personal referral.

Amy Schofield, ACRW • Schofield Strategies, LLC • schofieldstrategies.com

FRANK JORGENSEN

512-567-0890

frankjorgensen@gmail.com • **LinkedIn Profile**

April 17, 2017

Priscilla Hatton
General Manager
Hatton & Pierce Construction
43 Channel Center Street
Austin, TX 78708

Dear Ms. Hatton:

At the recommendation of Alan White, one of your long-time vendors, I am submitting my resume for consideration as your company's new **Construction Superintendent.**

To support your long-term business goals, I have the experience needed to supervise complex, unique projects with one-of-a-kind challenges. More important, I am a man on a passionate pursuit of good, quality work. My personal work philosophy can be summed up in these four ideas:

Practicality—Most of the time the best solution is the simplest solution that involves fewer people, fewer materials, and less time. My 23 years in the field have taught me the art of planning, short-cuts, work-arounds, and ingenious ways to get the job done—and done well.

Quality—My experience as a Real Estate Inspector has taught me to check out the fine points of construction that could cause quality issues in the future. I always fight for doing it right the first time.

Client Focus—I understand that every day of construction is a day the client is not in business. I stay in touch and work out small problems before they become big.

Safety—The men and women on my projects are taught safety practices, and I monitor follow-through. I believe ALL accidents are avoidable.

I love the business of construction and hope you will consider me as a member of your team. I will follow up within three days to arrange a time when we can meet in person.

Sincerely,

Frank Jorgensen

Resume attached

The clean, clear, easy-to-read style of this letter is appealing. While hitting on the hard skills and experience needed for the job, it also conveys a great deal about the job seeker's personal attributes—and relates those attributes to the benefits they bring to his company, his employees, and his clients.

Catherine Jewell, PCM • The Career Passion Coach • careerpassioncoach.com

VICTORIA LEE BREWSTER, BA

Oakville - ON - Canada   vicky-lee-brewster@rogers.com   416.823.9143

AWARD-WINNING SALES CONSULTANT | CLIENT SERVICES SPECIALIST

March 24, 2017

Ms. Julie Morgan
International Recruitment Manager
Holland America Line
777 Shipboard Lane
Seattle, WA 98118

Dear Ms. Morgan:

I have been referred to you by Carol Miller-Brown, a Registered Nurse in your Fleet Medical Operations unit. I've known Carol for many years, and she knows of my deep interest in a sales position with your cruise line.

Like Holland America, I have been honored with numerous awards and accolades recognizing my exemplary sales achievements and customer service attributes. The real estate sector is filled with sales representatives—some succeed and some don't. A commission-based sales career isn't for everyone, but I thrive in this environment.

My notable sales accomplishments include:

➢ **10-time President's Gold Award level** at Royal LePage—recognizing the top 5% of sales agents.

➢ **15 Master Sales Awards and an equal number of Sales Achievement Awards**; honestly too many to remember, as receiving them became the norm.

I lived in Ireland, France, Germany, and Switzerland before making Canada my home. I speak fluent French and understand the cultural norms unique to many different countries. I firmly believe my life experiences make me amply qualified to represent and fulfil the Holland America brand mission *to be the world's best hosts*.

I'm ready to join your vibrant team and board ship as a cruise sales consultant; all you have to do is call!

Sincerely,

Victoria Brewster

Resume attached

Customizing her letter to a specific company, this job seeker creates a clear link between prior experience and the roles she is targeting. She also draws in the reader by referring to the culture, slogan, and awards at the company she is hoping to join. The closing paragraph is jaunty and appropriate!

Brenda Collard-Mills, CRS • Robust Resumes & Resources • www.robustresumesandresources.com

From: **Anne Campbell,** acampbell47@yahoo.com
Subject: **Referred by Amos Lee**
Date: June 21, 2017
To: **Laura Lee-Croft,** leecroft.l@fourseasonswhistler.com

Hello, Laura—

I understand you're expecting my resume as your father has been quite the advocate for my joining your organization!

Let me give you a brief synopsis of why I'm a great fit.

- **My entire career has revolved around an innate ability to understand and delight the customer.** I have worked in both retail and administrative functions for high-profile consumer brands Booster Juice, Starbucks, and BMO.

- As Franchise Store Manager at Booster Juice, I direct all store operations on behalf of an in-absentia owner. Since 2014, **I have grown net sales, increased employee retention, and decreased spend.**

- At Starbucks, I oversaw the second-largest district store and **earned several peer-nominated commendations** for my unwavering dedication in **living the customer-focused brand values.**

I am amply qualified to fulfill a role involving many of your customer touchpoints and will do my utmost to cater to the clientele to ensure their stay is an unforgettable Four Seasons experience.

Your father speaks highly of your experience, sparking my interest in joining the Four Seasons brand. I look forward to an initial introduction via phone or Skype to explore how my retail management and customer service expertise will be best utilized in delighting the visitors and guests at Whistler.

I am excited to connect, as I have heard so much about you from one very proud father!

Sincerely,

Anne Campbell
>>>>>>>>>>>>>>>>>>

acampbell47@yahoo.com
Skype: AnneCampbell
Cell (call or text): 905-499-1479

This job seeker makes certain to mention her personal referral—the recipient's father—in the subject line, the opening sentence, and the final paragraph of her e-note. Although she's not applying for a specific job, she has identified several areas of the business where her skills will be of value.

Brenda Collard-Mills, CRS • Robust Resumes & Resources • www.robustresumesandresources.com

From: **Tige Medrano,** tmedrano@pobox.com
Subject: **Technical Recruiter** [Referred by Anju Gupta]
Date: February 3, 2017
To: **Bernie Danilo,** bernie.danilo@xtcdesign.com

Dear Mr. Danilo:

Anju Gupta, your Director of Regional Sales, recommended that I contact you regarding the opening you currently have for a Technical Recruiter. I supported recruiting efforts for Anju in her previous position, and she knows of my work ethic, relationship skills, and talent for uncovering "purple rabbits."

My professional qualifications include:

- Built and managed a $10 million business comprising 2 high-volume VMS accounts and 3 smaller non-VMS accounts.
- Built $6+ million business with a single client within the digital media space.
- Maintained a 3:1 interview:offer ratio.

My passion for helping candidates find rewarding career opportunities leads to drilling down to identify the right technical, cultural, and environmental fit. As a young and high-growth company, XTC Design would benefit greatly from the resulting decrease in turnover.

Impressed with what Anju has told me of the culture and vision at XTC, I have been interested in being a part of your continued growth for some time. I will follow up with you early next week to see if we can schedule a time to meet.

Sincerely,

Tige Medrano
217-354-3049
tmedrano@pobox.com
www.linkedin.com/in/tmedrano

This job seeker does more than just mention the person who referred him—he describes how they worked together in the past and what he has learned about the company from her, then relates that knowledge to how he can help the company. As a result, this letter is very personal, entirely customized, and extremely powerful.

Stephanie Swilley • TDM Associates • www.tdm-assoc.com

EMMA TURNER

555-456-6789 | emma.turner@yahoo.com
LinkedIn.com/in/EmmaTurner

January 10, 2017

Paul Dwyer— EVP, National Sales
Summit Financial Group
One Summit Drive
Montvale, NJ 07645

Re: Vice President, Northeast Region

Dear Paul:

In a recent conversation with Ken O'Hare and Bill Raymond, they recommended I contact you concerning your opening for a VP, Northeast, as I'm well qualified for the regional sales management role.

Over the past 18 months at Premiere Financial, I have worked nationwide with 300+ agents and brokers, streamlining operations and supporting efforts to market products, present to clients, and close deals. As a result, I quickly restored revenue growth for a region that had been without leadership for nearly 6 months.

The value I can provide to Summit includes:

- <u>Proven success in a competitive market</u>. I have excelled in the tough NYC-area market and can leverage established relationships at every level to support my team so they can sell.

- <u>Expertise in product education.</u> My talent for engaging and inspiring is a matter of record. I genuinely enjoy giving presentations, educating teams, and witnessing the results. I've presented to groups of 250+.

- <u>Tangible results.</u> As you know from both Ken and Bill, I consistently deliver in both up markets and down.

Are you available for a brief conversation Wednesday, January 18th? I have some ideas I'd like to discuss that are especially relevant to the Northeast. I will follow up in the next few days.

Sincerely,

Emma Turner

Attachment

This job seeker follows up a strong recommendation from 2 people with a letter that clearly yet concisely presents expert qualifications for the role. The centerpiece of the letter is the 3 bullet points, each expanding on a key qualification. Notice the promise of value in the closing paragraph—to share relevant ideas.

Marjorie Sussman, MRW, ACRW • www.visualcv.com/marjoriesussman

MILLICENT JAMES, MBA, BSMT (ASCP)

954.362.2219
millicentjames@outlook.com
Fort Lauderdale, FL 33316

Industry Authority on Patient-Centered Medical Home (PCMH) & Accountable Care Organization (ACO)

Deep Perspective of Healthcare Information Technology (HIT) & Leadership of Multimillion-Dollar Clinical Operations

June 17, 2017

Amanda Pierce
Chair, Board of Directors
Healthcare Data Corporation
222 Brickell Causeway
Miami, FL 33116

Dear Ms. Pierce:

Dr. Lyle Williams suggested I reach out to you to discuss the CEO search that the HDC board is currently conducting.

Lyle feels strongly that my leadership style and 16 years' experience in healthcare technology development and business building is "just what the doctor ordered" to help HDC expand its industry footprint and elevate its standing as a quality management solutions leader.

These achievements are a small sampling of strengths and value I bring to HDC:

- At IBN, I laid the groundwork to win a **$10M software licensing contract** with Aetna Insurance, then sparked **incremental $2M revenue** through a strategic partnership with our PCMH Community.

- As Director of Clinical Applications at Antonini Medical Center, I headed a **sweeping culture change,** partnering with C-suite leadership to compel **nationwide adoption of an electronic clinical platform.**

- At Norton Health, I drove **standardized installations for 15 hospitals in 4 years with no adverse effects.**

- I grew the Institute of Endocrinology lab business from **$0 to $3M+ annual revenues** and **2X its original size in 24 months** while deploying the infrastructure that earned it **coveted "Complex Laboratory" status.**

Rest assured, I can replicate similar results for HDC—driving strategic growth and realizing the market potential for your already strong products and technologies.

As an expert in ACO and PCMH initiatives, I have a vision for HDC's path to success and a product strategy to propel sales of your flagship solution. Let's set up a personal meeting this week so that we can discuss ideas and gain a better understanding of strategic priorities. I look forward to the start of many positive communications.

Sincerely,

Millicent James

"Millicent is the right person at the right time to take on a much more important role in driving the transformation we need in our healthcare system. She is the person to take you to the next level—really transform your business and bottom line!"
—**Dr. Peter Barrons, IBN Global Director of Healthcare Transformation**

The shaded segments of this cover letter draw the reader's eye to 3 strong elements: 1) a heading that defines the job seeker's expertise and brand; 2) specific achievements that demonstrate her value; and 3) a powerful endorsement that validates what she is saying about herself.

Sandra Ingemansen, CERM, CMRW, CPRW, CJSS • Resume Strategies • www.resume-strategies.com

CHAPTER 7:
Thank-You Letters

What Is a Thank-You Letter?

A thank-you letter is an essential component of every job seeker's arsenal. You'll send a thank-you letter after every interview and in other instances when someone has been helpful in your job search.

A letter sent after an interview does much more than say "thank you." It is a golden opportunity for you to reiterate the key points you made during the interview, further reinforce your value as a candidate, help you stand out, and remind your interviewer why you're such a good match for the position and the company.

And don't forget about recruiters. If you interviewed with a recruiter, it is just as important to send a thank-you letter as it is when you interviewed with a hiring manager or other company representative.

Other times, you will send a thank-you letter because someone has assisted you in some way. Perhaps a colleague made an introduction to someone on your behalf, helped you network with the right people, told you about an upcoming job opening, or otherwise put forth some effort for you. A thank-you letter recognizes that effort, keeps you top of mind with your contact, and creates tremendous good will.

> **Pro Tip: Don't underestimate the power of thank-you letters.** Believe it or not, many people never send thank-you letters. They either do not want to make the effort or do not understand the value and impact of these letters. Big mistake! Although we cannot guarantee you will get a job because you sent a thank-you letter, we can promise you that the letter will get you noticed and create a favorable impression.

What Do You Want to Achieve in Your Thank-You Letter?

Of course, your ultimate objective is to win a job offer. That's what this entire process is all about. But many companies require multiple interviews, so your objective early on might be simply to move your candidacy along and get a second or third interview … so you can then get the offer!

Beyond that ultimate objective, the purpose of your thank-you letter is to respond to what you learned at the interview about the company's "hot topics"—its needs, challenges, obstacles, opportunities, skills requirements, and other job-specific and company-specific details. Show that you listened, you learned, and you have what the company needs to meet that obstacle or conquer that challenge.

> **Pro Tip: Take notes during every interview so you know what's most important to each position and each company.** Refer to your notes when writing your thank-you letters so you're certain to hit the "hot spots" for your audience.

How Do You Write a Thank-You Letter?

In this chapter, we referred to 2 types of thank-you letters—the post-interview thank-you letter and the other that you send to acknowledge someone who has provided assistance with your search. The tone and style of these letters will be different; the information you include in them will be different.

Let's start with the post-interview thank-you note. Consider these possibilities for information to include:

- Work experience, job titles, employers, and/or educational credentials that very closely align with the job posting and were discussed during the interview.

- The most impressive achievements of your career as they relate directly to the challenges and opportunities the company or recruiter communicated during the interview. These are the things that the company needs to address immediately.

- The most relevant projects of your career. As with achievements, focus on projects that tie directly to what was discussed during the interview. Perhaps those projects were not really the most notable of your career. However, they are the most relevant to the company, and that is what matters most.

- Problems that you solved or helped solve—the same problems that the company is current facing.

- Opportunities that you captured or helped capture—similar to opportunities that the company is currently exploring.

- Other information that will demonstrate that you have what that company is looking for. Your unique value might include foreign language skills, international experience, technology expertise, military service, volunteer work, professional credentials, internships, student leadership activities, and much more. Every job seeker offers a unique portfolio of qualifications and experience. Reiterate yours in your thank-you letters as a reminder of why you are the perfect fit.

- Items of interest or particular note that you did not mention during the interview either because there was not enough time or you forgot to share them. It is never too late to send additional information that will further your candidacy.

The other type of thank-you letter that you will write is to acknowledge someone's assistance with your job search. This letter is easier and faster to write because it is written solely to express your appreciation and give that person an update on what has happened since you last connected.

Perhaps you got an interview and are waiting for an offer; maybe the contact you were referred to has introduced you to someone else; or a call opened doors at a company that is very difficult to penetrate. A quick thanks and brief update will keep your contact in the loop, again bring you top of mind, and let them know how much you appreciate their assistance … perhaps prompting them to offer even more!

Taking just a few minutes to write a quick e-note to someone who has made an effort on your behalf … that's just good manners and professional behavior.

How Do You Submit a Thank-You Letter?

You will send a thank-you letter as an e-note in an email message 99% of the time. As we have discussed throughout this book, there is no reason, particularly with a thank-you letter, to write a formal letter on letterhead. Instead, make it easy for the reader by writing your letter as the email message. It is quick and efficient and can easily be saved in email or in the database of a company or recruiter.

Send your post-interview thank-you letter immediately after an interview—either that day or the following day. The old expression of "strike while the iron is hot" is certainly true in this situation. You just had a great interview, so keep the positive energy flowing and create forward momentum.

For letters you are sending to people who have assisted in your search, we recommend that you still complete this task expediently, but it doesn't have to be instantly. If you want to set aside a day each week for composing and emailing those quick e-notes, that is fine.

Who Is the Audience?

Of course, the audience for thank-you letters is the people you have interviewed with. Do keep in mind, however, that others may read your letter. A manager might share it with his manager or someone in human resources. Any time you submit something in writing—to a company, a recruiter, or anyone else that you might reach out to during your search—know that others may be reading it.

That isn't a bad thing. In fact, it can be a good thing! If the manager you interviewed with is sharing your thank-you letter up the chain of command, you can feel somewhat confident that she is quite interested in making you an offer.

The personal thank-you letter that you send to acknowledge someone's assistance is private communication between you and that person. Chances are that no one else will see it.

To Whom Do You Send It?

As already mentioned, send a thank-you letter to anyone who interviewed you or helped you in some way with your job search.

If you interviewed with multiple people at a certain company, take the time to email an individual thank-you note to each person. Each letter should be a bit different, focusing on the items that seemed most important to that particular person.

What Are the Unique Characteristics of a Thank-You Letter?

On the following pages, we share with you 10 powerful thank-you letters—letters that capture the essence of an interview, reiterate the candidate's strongest points, and express enthusiasm for the company and the position. What you will notice is how different they are in style and substance. The box at the bottom of each page gives specific notes about that letter.

JOHN QUINCY ROBINSON
linkedin.com/in/johnqrobinson • 203-342-5552 • johnquincyrobinson@gmail.com

July 7, 2016

Ms. Susan Lopez
Milford Medical Supplies
1818 Peachtree Boulevard
Milford, CT 06460-6713

Dear Ms. Lopez:

Thank you for taking the time to speak with me yesterday at the Trumbull Job Fair. I appreciated learning about Milford Medical Supplies and the position of Client Service Representative.

As I mentioned during our conversation, I offer Milford Medical Supplies:

- ✓ 12+ years of experience in an identical capacity at Nutmeg Medical Supplies.
- ✓ An extensive background in both customer service and vendor relations.
- ✓ An Associate's Degree in Business Management.

During our conversation, you noted that you and members of the candidate review committee will be making a decision within the next few weeks. Please let me know if I can provide any additional information to further my candidacy.

In the interim, I encourage you to also visit my LinkedIn profile for additional details about my qualifications along with 10 endorsements from previous supervisors, vendors, and customers.

I am confident that my professional experience and forte for providing outstanding customer service will enable me to be an asset to Milford Medical Supplies. Thank you again for your time and consideration.

Cordially,

John Q. Robinson

A notable feature of this thank-you letter is a reference to the job seeker's LinkedIn profile (in next-to-last paragraph) with live link for a 1-click connection to 10 third-party recommendations—powerful endorsements! The 3 bullet points reinforce his "perfect match" to the most important requirements discussed at the interview.

Ross Primack, CPRW, CEIP, GCDF • Connecticut Department of Labor • www.ctdol.state.ct.us

Sheila Peters

963.521.8754 ◆ Boston, MA 02115
Linkedin/in/sheilapbostonma ◆ shelia24@hotmail.com

ADMINISTRATIVE SPECIALIST
Customer Service | Web Design | Social Media

March 17, 2017

Sarah H. Mills, President
Logo Designz Web, Inc.
Boston, MA 02115

Dear Ms. Mills:

Thank you for sharing your time to discuss your company, Logo Designz Web, Inc., during our informational interview on March 15th. As a well-qualified **administrative professional**, I have proven talents in office administration in addition to expertise in web design, marketing, social media, and customer service, and I would love to put these to work for your company.

Most recently, I delivered broad-based administrative support to Fister Corporation, a family-owned dry cleaning business with zero social media capabilities in 2016. In this role, I communicated with customers and vendors and built a loyal following through social media, resulting in a **50% increase** in garments cleaned weekly by January 2017.

Additional highlights of the value I have brought to past employers include …

- ◆ Increasing profitability by bringing an efficient and client-friendly approach to accounts receivable operations.

- ◆ Collaborating on the design of an upgraded website, using my innate creativity to develop customer profiles to increase usability.

- ◆ Maintaining high-quality, high-touch relationships with customers and vendors, always promoting swift issue resolution and prompt and attentive follow-through.

As you can see, I possess the diverse background in administration and website operations needed to efficiently support your organization. In addition, I can work on-site, as I live within walking distance of your office. I look forward to speaking with you again about this opportunity. Thank you!

Sincerely,

Sheila Peters

This job seeker is using her thank-you letter to transition from informational interview to job application. She shares an example of how she helped another small company and then reinforces her top skills. In the closing paragraph she mentions an intangible that could be valuable—her close proximity to the business.

Sophia Marshall, MHR, ACRW, BCC • Me Sheet • www.mesheet.com

From: **Sandy Squiller,** sandy@squiller.com
Subject: **Thank you — Further thoughts — Core values**
Date: April 2, 2017
To: **Richard Jones,** richard.jones@baggottagency.com

Richard,

Thank you for speaking with me on Friday about the Manager Partnership Strategy and Service position.

I enjoyed our conversation and look forward to the possibility of joining the team during this exciting restructuring. I am a big believer in your vision to transform the Partnerships group into an internal agency and would love to be a part of the implementation. My past experience shows that I encompass the core values you seek in candidates for this position:

—Committed to improve every day:
Selected to participate in a 10-week WorldGroup training program for high-potential junior-level talent.

—Exude passion:
Identified sports sponsorship as the area of interest for my career and secured positions with key players in the niche field (Octagon and Momentum).

—Integrity (do things the right way, even if it's the hard way):
Implemented sponsorship asset-tracking process for various American Express Business Units.

—Outwork everyone:
Lured recruits from other university fraternities to recruit largest new member class in my fraternity's history.

—Intensity, effort, productivity:
Promoted from Assistant Account Executive to Account Executive after one year at Momentum (this jump typically takes two years).

I will stay in touch with HR regarding the hiring process. In the meantime, please let me know if you have any further questions about my background and experience.

Best,

Sandy
>=>=>=>=>=>=
Sandy Squiller
sandy@squiller.com
213-670-3900

This letter showcases an excellent follow-up strategy: Connect the job seeker's skills and experience to the precise needs discussed at the interview. Notice how each "core value" is followed with a specific example to reinforce a strong fit with the position, the organization, and—just as importantly—the culture.

Eric Kramer • InterviewBest • www.interviewbest.com

From: **Jesse O. Maxwell,** Maxwell.Jesse@yahoo.com
Subject: **Senior Systems Specialist—Thank you and further details**
Date: June 24, 2017
To: **Ronald Hart,** hart_ron@digitalservices.com

Dear Mr. Hart:

It was a pleasure meeting with you last Friday to elaborate on my wealth of experience as well as my interest in joining your team as a Senior Systems Specialist. Your organization's goals are simply outstanding, and it would be my pleasure to help you achieve them.

As we discussed, I offer strong experience and qualifications for this position:

- **Project Management:** In my current role I am known as "master multi-tasker," keeping numerous projects moving forward by carefully managing budgets, internal communications, and deadlines.
- **Web Design Experience:** Although principally a programmer, I managed the corporate website redesign at my prior company and completed the project (to rave reviews) on time and on budget.
- **Technical Knowledge:** I have completed training in ITIL, Foundations, CITAM, CSAM, CHAMP, CITAD, HDI SCTL, HDI SCA, HDI DST, MCSA, Network+, A+, WAN, LAN, Windows 95, 98, NT, 2000, XP, UNIX 8.5, and MAC OX 10.X.

I remain highly interested in joining your team and would be honored to proceed to the next steps in the hiring process. I am confident that my strong work ethic, quality focus, and passion for process improvement will make me a positive asset to your organization and staff members alike.

I look forward to hearing from your team to discuss next steps. Meanwhile, if I can provide you with any additional information, please do not hesitate to contact me.

Best regards—

Jesse O. Maxwell
361-876-1067
Maxwell.Jesse@yahoo.com

Bold headings make the bullet points stand out—and that's helpful, because they contain an excellent recap of the job seeker's qualifications and experiences as they relate to the position. The bullets emphasize value and results as well as very important technical expertise.

Zakiyyah Mussallihullah, CPRW, CPCC • Customized Resume Writing Services • eslexclusive@gmail.com

JOHN J. HORN

IDEAS ⇨ ACTION ⇨ RESULTS

832-123-4567 | Katy, TX 77494 | johnjhorn@comcast.net | www.linkedin.com/in/johnjhorn

January 5, 2017

Mr. Mark Kaplan
Tangerine Promotions
900 Skokie Blvd., Suite 275
Houston, TX 77005

Dear Mr. Kaplan:

Thank you for your time on Tuesday and for sharing your insights about the opportunity with Tangerine Promotions. In anticipation of our next meeting, I have given considerable thought to the position, your expectations for growth, and the challenges inherent in the role. To that end, I would like to bring a few key points to the forefront:

⇨ Leading a branding effort is something I have done for 3 different companies. All were successful and some have seen sales growth in excess of 500% after the new brand was launched.

⇨ Social media can't be ignored in today's marketplace. Even in the energy industry, where you don't think of social media being relevant, I was able to build the second-largest following for any electricity utility in just a year. This experience can help Tangerine Promotions accelerate its online presence.

⇨ My most recent experience has been in the energy industry, and prior to that in telecommunications and entertainment, so I truly view myself as industry agnostic. The key to gaining market share is delivering products and offers that are relevant to your customers. I am confident I can get up to speed on the promotional product industry in no time to execute campaigns that will boost revenues.

I look forward to moving to the next step in your selection process. Thank you again for your time and consideration.

Sincerely,

John J. Horn

Much more than a "thank-you-for-the-interview" message, this letter reiterates key value points and relates them to the needs of the company as explored during the interview. The letter is concise and to the point. Notice the attractive "Ideas—Action—Results" letterhead that further highlights the job seeker's core abilities.

Michelle Robin, NCRW, CPRW • Brand Your Career • www.brandyourcareer.com

KATIE CARUSO

Chicago, IL 60615 • 773-644-3567 • kcaruso@yahoo.com

March 10, 2017

Todd Johnson
FEMA 5-MSD-ASB Branch Chief
536 S. Clark, 6th Floor
Chicago, IL 60605

Dear Mr. Johnson:

I would like to give a sincere thank-you to you and your team for interviewing me on Thursday. I enjoyed learning about the position and welcome the opportunity to become a member of the Mission Support Division. The position seems a perfect fit, allowing me to put my 12 years of financial and accounting experience to good use in supporting FEMA's important work.

Some key points I would like to emphasize:

➢ I am highly flexible with **no time or location restraints.** I am not bound by geographical region, so assisting out in the field with floods and disasters would not be a problem for me.

➢ As your Disaster Spend Coordinator, I can offer a record of **100% accuracy** in handling travel expenses, billing, and invoicing in my 3 past positions (Client Finance with DDB, Business Manager for TARTA USA, and Budget Project Manager for OMD).

➢ My creative problem-solving skills are also very strong. Whether responding to an upset client or switching gears due to unforeseen obstacles, I remain calm and **handle stressful situations** with the utmost professionalism.

You may also be interested in knowing that I will sit for my CPA exam next month. This, along with my experience, will enable me to be an even greater asset to your high-performance workforce.

Thank you again for considering me for the Financial Management Specialist position. I look forward to joining the FEMA organization.

Sincerely,

Katie Caruso

The 3 bullet points highlight qualifications that are closely related to the position—representing technical skills (finance and accounting), personal attributes (ability to deal with stressful situations), and flexibility (no geographic restraints). In working for FEMA, all 3 of these will be essential!

Wendy Steele, CPRW • BluePrint Resumes and Consulting • www.blueprintresumes.com

Steven K. Stiffler

Long Beach, CA 90806 / LinkedIn Profile   **(310) 292-7380 / stifflersk999@aol.com**

January 1, 2017

Tom Tryon, Director of Manufacturing
Fluor Corporation Headquarters
6700 Las Colinas Blvd.
Irving, TX 75039

Dear Mr. Tryon:

Thank you for interviewing me on Friday. We discussed my dual Masters in Business and Engineering as well as my 20-year history in aerospace manufacturing technologies, where I **managed multimillion-dollar engineering contracts and budgets, product lines, and large workforces** at:

~ **Northrop Aircraft:** Manufacturing Engineering Manager, 5 years and Business Development Manager, 2 years;
~ **Valley Todeco:** Manufacturing Manager, 3 years;
~ **Industrial Tectonics:** Manufacturing Engineering Manager, 3 years;
~ **Thomas & Betts Bowers:** Manufacturing Manager, 2 years; and
~ **Chalco Engineering, Inc.:** Manufacturing Engineer, 5 years.

Not only did I exceed ROI goals—delivering millions of dollars in cost reductions, workforce efficiency, and automation improvements—but I demonstrated astute business acumen and manufacturing expertise.

For example, I …

➢ Launched profitable, lean manufacturing cells and several new product lines at 3 companies; and
➢ Spearheaded and conducted successful plant-wide training, quality improvement programs, and Kaizen events that resulted in efficiency improvements and cost reductions.

And delivered significant numbers …

➢ Fast payback of less than 2 years for high-value capital equipment acquisitions;
➢ Man-hour reductions of more than 15% and average throughput time of 30%; and
➢ Scrap rate reductions of 75% over 10 months.

I look forward to discussing more of my business and engineering solutions with you soon.

Warmest wishes,

Steven K. Stiffler

P.S. Here's the link for that Callaway driver I mentioned: http://www.callawaygolf.com/golf-clubs/drivers-2016-xr.html

With 3 sections of bullet points, this letter is well organized and easy to skim. The job seeker reiterates his overall qualifications and key accomplishments—with impressive numbers. Notice the P.S., where he follows up on a personal topic discussed during the interview. That is an excellent technique to bond with the interviewer.

Roleta Fowler Vasquez, CPRW • Wordbusters Resume Service • www.wordbustersresumeandwritingservices.com

JOHN W. SORGEN

914-877-9090 ▪▪ johnwsorgen@comcast.net ▪▪ Croton, NY 96718
www.linkedin.com/in/johnwsorgen

March 4, 2017

Mr. William Laramie
Curran Executive Search
345 Third Avenue
New York, NY 20041

Dear Mr. Laramie:

The Division Sales Manager position we discussed today is a perfect fit between my qualifications and your client company's need for a sales leader who will set and consistently surpass the bar for top performance.

A few examples…

Providing Strong Leadership + Hands-on Sales Team Management = Results
- Recruited and led team to drive sales from 5% to 52% growth in 3 product categories in 10 months.
- Doubled distributor base, drove sales 150%, and achieved 67% sales growth in a highly competitive market.

Developing Strategic Business Plans + Skilled Contract Negotiations = Results
- Tripled sales to $162.5M in 3 years by focusing on large accounts and launching new marketing campaigns.
- Improved product displays across account base and negotiated a 25% discount on service contracts.

Effective Merchandising Programs + Driving Sales through Brand Reinforcement = Results
- Grew product line sales of a $14M account by $33M in 12 months.
- Ranked #1 in sales, generating 43% of revenues region-wide.

I look forward to meeting with your client next week and discussing how I can lead their sales turnaround.

Sincerely,

John W. Sorgen

Recapping key sales results creates a very strong letter that will resonate with the recruiter and his client company seeking a great sales person. Note how tightly the letter is written—everything is on 1 or 2 lines for easy reading, and the bold, creative headings send a repeated message of "results."

Louise Garver, CERM, CPRW, CJSS, CPBS • Career Directions, LLC • careerdirectionsllc.com

From: **Samuel C. Oats,** samcoats@rr.com
Subject: **Communications Security (COMSEC) Manager Employment Opportunity**
Date: 17 June 2017
To: **Mary Evans,** mary.evans@communicationssecurityllc.com

Ms. Evans—

Thank you for the opportunity to interview with you and the search committee for the contract position of **COMMUNICATIONS SECURITY (COMSEC) MANAGER** at the White House Communications Agency on Bolling Air Force Base in Washington, DC.

Allow me to provide you with what I consider to be some compelling food for thought to support why I am the ideal candidate for the position.

POSITION-SPECIFIC OCCUPATIONAL MILESTONES

- I was honored by being selected over 85 colleagues to become a member of the elite White House Communications Agency team tasked to support the President, First Lady, and Vice President; US Secret Service; and senior White House staff, and to safeguard highly sensitive communication security assets valued at $126M.

LEADERSHIP OFFERINGS

- As a hands-on, highly communicative manager, I use *leadership, cooperation, communication,* and *commitment* (LC$_3$) principles to achieve desired outcomes. I convey information—whether designed for long-range impact or to resolve short-term situations—in an effective and appropriate manner. My decisive yet people-centric brand of leadership promotes teamwork and loyalty.

I look forward to the next steps in the selection process and will follow up this week to see if any questions have arisen since our meeting. Again, thank you.

Respectfully,

Samuel C. Oats
240-123-4568
samcoats@rr.com
LinkedIn Profile

> Most notable about this thank-you letter is the format: Big, bold headlines are followed by high-level and very impressive information supporting the key qualifications for the position. The job title is also heavily bolded in the first paragraph as well as in the subject line.

Phyllis Houston • The Resume Expert • www.rezxprt.com

CHARLES ANDERSON

531.814.8923

CHARLES.ANDERSON@GMAIL.COM

CHARLESANDERSON.COM | LINKEDIN.COM/IN/CHARLESANDERSON

INDIANAPOLIS, IN

March 21, 2017

Stan Smith
Chief Executive Officer
Business Solutions, LLC

> *"We were in the red when Charles came on board. I don't know how he managed it, but his solutions cost us next to nothing. He knew exactly what to do, where to be, and what to change. In just 18 months, he turned us around. We just broke the $100M mark—and it's because of Charles."*
>
> **— Emily Johnson**, Founder and CEO of tech startup *OmniMin*

COST REDUCER ■ PEOPLE MOTIVATOR ■ SENIOR TECH EXECUTIVE EXTRAORDINAIRE

As discussed in our recent phone call, Stan, I am ready to tackle a new challenge and craft a roadmap to a successful future for Business Solutions, LLC. A few examples of success we spoke only briefly about include:

■ **DOING MORE WITH LESS:** As Director of Technology for *Artnen, Inc.*, I reduced my budget from $20M to $8M through infrastructure reconfiguration, while never losing sight of quality ... which improved by 25% over 2 years. This was the first time I worked myself out of a position, an achievement I am proud of to this day.

■ **LIGHTING TEAMS' FIRES:** In more than 6 roles, I mentored and motivated several senior-level managers who were struggling with their positions. Turning around their attitude and skills helped transform their groups, resulting in a combined total of $50M+ in additional revenue ... all through the power of motivation.

■ **"PULLING A CHARLES":** My previous role as CTO of *Hanaito Marketing* saw several obstacles during the JV and subsequent merging of offices. I inspired a spirit of collaboration among the new management teams, relieved tension, and gained consensus for new processes. This is now known across the company as "pulling a Charles."

Stan, our past collaboration enabled the success of my previous employer, and I truly look forward to the opportunity to work with you again. I will call you on March 26 so we can wrap up the discussion of my vision for your company's IT and IS success. Thank you for your time, and I'll speak with you again in a few days!

Sincerely,

Charles Anderson

This thank-you letter follows up a recent conversation and a long-standing relationship, so the tone is a bit less formal than many. The quote and tagline at the top create a powerful introduction, and the bullet points offer pertinent examples that illustrate this job seeker's unique value.

Laura Gonzalez, ACRW, CPRW • Masterwork Resumes • www.masterworkresumes.com

CHAPTER 8:

Letters for Challenging Job Search Situations

This chapter is all about writing job search letters when you have unique challenges and/or circumstances impacting your quest for employment. We share strategies and samples in 6 categories:

- Career Changers
- Military Transition Personnel
- Military Spouse and/or Volunteer
- Ex-Offenders
- LGBTQ Individuals
- Immigrants

Career Changers

Career change is the job search challenge that is the most common, affecting people who are seeking to shift career paths, professions, and/or industries. Some changes are minor, such as moving from consumer goods sales into technology sales, while others can be much more significant—such as transitioning from a UFC fighter into a career in shipping and receiving, as you will read in one of the letters in this section.

Career change happens frequently in today's modern world of work. In generations past, people entered a career field and stayed in that field, working for the same company, for years … for decades. Today, that is the exception to the rule. People now move more fluidly from one industry to another and from one profession to another to meet changing workforce demands.

Workers today also tend to be much more conscious of work/life balance and personal/professional fulfillment. As baby boomers age and start moving out of the workforce, younger generations do not view work in the same way. In fact, they consider it almost commonplace to make career shifts—from small to massive—as a routine part of their working lives.

> **Pro Tip: If you are moving from one profession to another or one industry to another, career change letters will be an essential component of your job search toolkit.** When writing your letters or your resume, keep your objective front and center in your mind so you are showcasing what is important to your *new* career path and not just summarizing experiences and successes from years past. Let your objective drive the entire writing process!

Let's closely examine 4 letters written for very different career change situations. Take the lessons from these letters and apply them to yours—as appropriate—so your letters focus on your relevant skills, qualifications, and achievements and not on the fact that you are changing careers. Readers will figure that out themselves.

Alex Zordakis Letter—Page 153

How often do you see a turkey on a job search letter? Not too often! But it is perfect for Alex's situation. And doesn't it capture your attention immediately—precisely its purpose?

As you read Alex's letter, you instantly understand the reason for the turkey. He is writing to a company that supplies turkeys and other food supplies to restaurants. In fact, Alex has been a long-time customer of the company to which he is writing.

In the first paragraph he powerfully explains why he's writing, attributing the quality of Galveston Purveyors' products and services to the success of his restaurant. That is a great way to start a conversation—with honest and positive feedback that will instantly make the president proud of his company's achievements.

The opening also communicates that Alex is familiar with the company's products, instantly setting himself apart from others who may have sales experience but not the same familiarity with this particular company. In the second paragraph, he makes a further connection by mentioning the name of the Galveston Purveyors employee who manages his account and who notified him about the sales position.

In paragraph 3, Alex shares his specific skills as they relate to the sales position he is targeting. He then pulls it all together by writing about his vast knowledge of restaurant operations, valuable knowledge because that is the clientele he will sell to and service. He truly is the perfect candidate for this position.

When you read this letter, you do not even notice that it's a career change, but it is a big one—moving from daily restaurant operations into field sales. However, the letter is written in such a manner that everything is connected and it seems like a seamless transition.

Marie Cannon Letter—Page 154

Marie's letter is a perfect example of an e-note—short, concise, and to the point, and used as the actual content of an email message.

As you read, you will see that Marie wants to transition from her wedding planning business into technology sales, a big shift in profession, yet still servicing the same industry. Who better to sell WEDDINGAPP to wedding and event planners than someone who has used the app to do that specific job?

The letter begins with a great strategy—acknowledging the company, its press coverage, and its track record of growth. Everyone likes positive feedback, even young tech entrepreneurs. It goes one step further and lets the reader know that Marie has used the application—almost daily—for the past 6 months. Again, who better to sell the product than a current user?

Alex Zordakis
Lakeshore Grill
2656 Center Street
Houston, TX 77013

(713) 898-3667

alex@lakeshoregrill.com

May 14, 2017

Mr. Luke Conrad, President
Galveston Purveyors
555 Jackson Trail
Galveston, TX 77550

Dear Luke:

Let's talk turkey!

For many years you have known me as one of your best customers for the high-quality meat and poultry products that Galveston Purveyors has provided to my restaurant. My son is now taking over this hugely popular business, whose success is due in large part to your prompt deliveries of the right orders, in the right quantities, at the right price.

I am now free to pursue a passion of mine—**restaurant food sales**—so I am very much interested in the **Territory Manager** position I learned about from Charlie Simmons, who services my account. Having been exposed to every aspect of restaurant operations from an early age, I know this career change will be a natural progression for me.

My strong commitment to quality and service, combined with heavy experience in marketing, customer/vendor relations, personnel development, cash/inventory control, and menu enhancements, would serve me well in selling your food products to restaurant owners/chefs. They can benefit from my vast knowledge of the industry to increase their profitability potential.

As your account representative, I am positive I would be able to contribute to achieving or exceeding your goals. I am excited to discuss this opportunity in more detail and will call next week to set a time to meet.

Thank you,

Alex Zordakis

Resume attached

Melanie Noonan • Peripheral Pro LLC • PeriPro1@aol.com

From:	**Marie Cannon,** marie@specialtyweddingsllc
Subject:	**Very happy customer with an idea for you!**
Date:	March 30, 2017
To:	**Todd Lee,** todd.lee@weddingapp.com

Hi Todd,

I found your contact information on Facebook and wanted to reach out to congratulate you on your recent article in the *Baton Rouge Business Report*.

It does not surprise me that WEDDINGAPP is a success not only here locally but gaining popularity nationwide. I downloaded it six months ago and have been using it almost daily to help me in my wedding planning business. In fact, I have some innovative ideas that could help your app reach even more users.

It would be my dream job to share my unique combination of

- marketing knowledge
- event planning experience
- social media savvy

… to offer WEDDINGAPP a solid trifecta.

Please take a look at my attached resume. I hope you are as excited as I am about the possibility of working together to enhance your brand and *revolutionize the wedding planning industry*.

All the best,

Marie Cannon
Specialty Weddings, LLC
Baton Rouge, LA
marie@specialtyweddingsllc
www.specialtyweddings2llc.com
225-333-2126

In just 6 short words, Marie tells the reader everything he needs to know about her skills in marketing, event planning, and social media. Because it is presented in a bulleted format, the information is eye-catching and easy to skim. She has a *solid trifecta* of qualifications, as she notes.

Her short, final paragraph is engaging and exciting as she writes about *revolutionizing the wedding planning industry.* We can assume this phrase ties directly to the company's mission statement. Perfect letter … perfect length … perfect skills … perfect candidate fit.

Martin Babcock Letter—Page 156

Martin's letter is another strong example of how to segue from one career into a totally different career path. Martin is the UFC fighter mentioned earlier in this section—the person who now wants to work as a shipping associate. This is quite a stretch, but he connects the two seamlessly in his job search letter. How does he accomplish that?

- In the first paragraph, Martin immediately addresses the core skills required of a shipping associate—someone who is agile, is physically strong, can think on his feet, and performs as a team player. He then tells the reader he is *all that and more!*

- Knowing that there are probably not many UFC fighters applying for the same job, he uses that information to his advantage by bringing it to the forefront in the second paragraph.

- More importantly, he then shares 3 bullet points that correlate his experience with the skills required for the position. He makes a solid connection between what he has done in the past and how that relates directly to the advertised job posting.

- To add a bit of zest to the letter, Martin references his ability to tackle shipping containers as an easier opponent than those who challenged him in the ring. That makes his letter even more engaging and entertaining, while still supporting that he is well qualified.

- The letter closes with an immediate call to action—*Call me!* The remainder of that paragraph again connects the two diverse career paths, and it works. If you were hiring for a shipping associate, wouldn't you take the time to interview this most unusual, yet seemingly qualified, candidate?

McKenzie Taylor Letter—Page 157

In the final sample career change letter, you meet McKenzie, an attorney who has recently relocated and is looking for a new career opportunity. McKenzie's more formal-looking job search letter is an appropriate visual presentation for an individual in her career field. Of course, she could have used an e-note, but the letterhead itself communicates a message of professionalism while the content in the letterhead clearly defines her brand as it aligns with her targeted position in community empowerment.

The first paragraph communicates why McKenzie is writing—she has just moved to New York City, did her research to identify the top organizations that could utilize her professional skills, and identified The Maisley Foundation as one of those. Even more to the point, she found a job posting for a Program Director with that organization.

From: **Martin Babcock,** martinbabcock@telus.net
Subject: **Shipping Associate—Posting #SA-2016-35**
Date: April 16, 2017
To: **Jackie Cranson,** jackiecranson@weshipit.com

Dear Ms. Cranson:

The job of Shipping Associate requires someone who is agile, physically strong, and can think on their feet but also perform as a trusted team player. I am that and more!

You may wonder how a freshly retired UFC fighter will fit into your corporate culture and fulfill the job duties. Let me explain.

➢ The demands of my profession required me to remain **mentally calm and physically strong** to compete and hold my ground against some of the world's top-ranked fighters.

➢ As a personal trainer, I'm known for my **attentive customer service**.

➢ My involvement in sports has instilled three key skills: **discipline, responsibility, and ethics**.

I would now rather make full contact with shipping containers than grappling with an opponent in the ring!

Call me and give me a chance to show you my readiness to pack boxes with the same precision I used to pack a punch.

Sincerely,

Martin Babcock
martinbabcock@telus.net
416.997.4293

McKenzie **Taylor**

(917) 222-0555 • New York, NY

Mc.Taylor@gmail.com

}

Public Affairs

Breaking barriers with a commitment to community empowerment

February 8, 2017

Mary Ann Nichols
HR Director
The Maisley Foundation
62 Broadway
New York, NY 10005

Dear Ms. Nichols:

Being new to the New York area, I hit the ground running to research top organizations that could utilize my unique background in both law and community service. The Maisley Foundation made that list, so I was excited to see your posting for a Program Director on Idealist.

As an attorney, I spent nights preparing briefs and developing new initiatives, and I gave more oral arguments than I'd dare to count. However, I still remember the major impact of tutoring student-athletes in college. With that one opportunity, the seed for community empowerment was planted.

Through my experiences, I have honed many skills that will allow me to support the mission of your organization. Some you may find relevant include:

✓ **Developed and refined environmental policies,** streamlining existing frameworks 22%.

✓ **Collaborated with environmental specialists** to rework community programs, resulting in 14% improvement in air quality.

✓ **Won 97% of all cases** against corporate companies making environmental violations.

I look forward to meeting with you to discuss the opportunity and my qualifications in detail. To expedite the process, I will call your office on Monday to schedule a time that's convenient for you.

 Sincerely,

McKenzie Taylor

Enclosure: Resume

Next up in the letter is a brief summary of her experience as an attorney, along with an explanation of her first venture into community activism and empowerment. This makes for a very strong connection with the advertised position.

The third paragraph, introducing McKenzie's 3 core achievements most related to the job she is pursuing, effectively uses bold print to draw the reader's attention to the information that is most important—environmental policy expertise, collaboration skills, and courtroom success. With these facts, she communicates that she has what it takes to perform well for Maisley.

The final paragraph is a tastefully assertive closing. As we've recommended, don't leave your career under others' control! Take the initiative and work to move yourself from applicant to interviewee.

Military Transition Personnel

People who have served our nation and are now transitioning from the military to the civilian world of work have unique issues to address when writing their job search letters and resumes. Fortunately, most of these individuals have overcome numerous obstacles, so managing a job search—if done well—should be relatively efficient and productive.

One of the most important things to keep in mind when writing military-to-civilian transition letters is the audience. Your approach will be distinctly different when writing to civilian companies versus military and/or government contractors.

- **When writing to civilian companies, put the heaviest emphasis on your skills, experiences, educational credentials, and achievements.** You might mention your record of military service, but it should be secondary to your talent portfolio—the things that matter most to that company.

- **When writing to quasi-government agencies and government/military contractors, both things matter—your talent portfolio and your military service.** Put an equal emphasis on both by mentioning your knowledge of military organizations, operations, regulations, processes, and other details that align with your employment targets.

> **Pro Tip: Do not write about "transferrable skills."** Instead, write about your skills and qualifications and how you can use them to the benefit of your targeted employer. You OWN those skills, so there's no transferring involved! You are just going to do what you already do—albeit in a different environment.

As you review the 4 military-to-civilian transition letters that follow, it's important to understand:
- *How* each letter was written.
- *Why* it was written in a particular style.
- *What* information was highlighted and why it was the most important.

All of those decisions were made based on the specific employer that each job seeker was targeting.

John Jacobs Letter—Page 160

John's letter is somewhat formal in its structure and has more content than many of the other letters in this book. However, it is perfect for him and his situation. He has had a long and distinguished military career, and he wants to showcase elements of his career that align specifically with his targeted position of Administrative Specialist.

It is very important to note that much of what is highlighted in this letter aligns directly with the job posting. First, the advertisement encouraged military personnel to apply; thus, in his very first sentence John mentions his 9 years of service with the USMC. The rest of that paragraph addresses the company's need for *delivering operational support, training new personnel, managing in 24/7 environments,* and *multitasking.*

The letter then uses what we refer to as a *functional style*—skill headings, in bold, followed by short paragraphs summarizing the candidate's relevant experience. The 3 skill sets highlighted in this letter were precisely the core qualifications (also known as keywords) in the job posting. The reader can quickly skim and instantly identify that the candidate has the requisite qualifications.

Also included in those 3 skill sections are John's most notable achievements as they relate to the targeted job. He communicates an important message—not only does he have the skills and experience, but he also delivers results in each of those critical areas. Achievements strengthen the impact of this and every job search letter.

John closes with an explanation of why he is in the job market by mentioning that his service with the USMC is coming to an end. Then, in a professional yet proactive method, he asks for the interview and alerts the reader to the fact that he will be following up. Great close!

Ashley Meadows Letter—Page 161

Ashley's letter is an outstanding example of 5 characteristics of a great job search letter:

- **It is a modern e-note,** written in a short and concise style and used as the body of the email message. It is modern in both appearance and content.

- **It showcases notable career achievements,** all of which are valuable in the corporate world. Ashley has saved money, improved efficiency, increased output, and enhanced customer service. Even before you get to the real content of the letter, you are engaged and want to know more.

- **It drives readers to read the resume,** with numerous references to the valuable information contained there. This strategy will work only if you have shared some notable achievements in the letter so readers are already interested.

- **It explains her interest in this particular company in this particular location.** Ashley shares that Corinth, a small town in Vermont, is her hometown, and that she would rather work at a small company that values its customers as opposed to a large organization. Is that information essential? No, but it does make her a "local" with a strong connection to the company and the community, and that can give her a distinct advantage.

JOHN C. JACOBS

San Diego, CA 92114 ▪ (c) 858.662.1009 ▪ (e) johnjacobs24@mac.com

ADMINISTRATIVE PROFESSIONAL
Management Support / Operations Management / Process Improvement

April 5, 2017

Ms. Mary Leverett
Director of Human Resources
Enterprise Logistics, LLC
862 South Park Avenue
Temecula, CA 96231

Dear Ms. Leverett:

After 9 years within the USMC, I am applying to the **Administrative Specialist** position with your organization. Throughout my career I have delivered administrative support and trained new military recruits while managing operations within fast-paced 24/7 environments across multiple hazardous duty locations. I am an expert at multitasking, a key characteristic of successful administrators.

During my time in the USMC, I've developed strong skills that can benefit your company. Specifically:

Management Support: My ability to maintain flawless administrative oversight of projects, schedules, and budgets has repeatedly been recognized by my superiors. In fact, I have a reputation for always being ahead of schedule and always surpassing quality objectives.

Operations Management: Having worked for the largest command within the USMC, I was relied on to oversee performance evaluation processes for 1K+ military members. This included managing career progression and coordinating professional development. Under my tenure, 25% of military members utilized tuition assistance. This was a 10% increase from the previous year.

Process Improvement: As an instructor, ensuring quality instruction was my #1 priority. I highlighted training inconsistencies and developed courses to address issues. In one case, I boosted data accuracy by championing the migration of 400+ annual training reports into an online tracking system.

Ms. Leverett, I am the administrative expert who can support the needs of Enterprise Logistics, LLC. I am enthusiastic about the potential of meeting with you to discuss the value I offer your organization and will call early next week in hopes of scheduling a meeting. Thank you.

Sincerely,

John C. Jacobs

Enclosure: Resume

Sophia Marshall, MHR, ACRW, BCC • Me Sheet • www.mesheet.com

From: **Ashley Meadows,** almeadows@hotmail.com
Subject: **Bringing Profit-Building Capabilities to Apex**
Date: January 9, 2017
To: **Charles W. Moran,** cwmoran@apexllc.com

Dear Mr. Moran:

**Saved $175K ... efficiency up 40% ... output jumped 400% ...
customers much better served ... retained a very valuable team member**

You've just seen some of the value I delivered to customers at least as demanding as yours. You'll find even more in my attached resume, tailored to help you find your next General Manager.

That document may not look like others you've scanned. Right at the top are 8 profit-building capabilities I want to put at Apex's disposal from day 1. Backing them up are nearly a dozen examples of costs cut, brands expanded, customers better served, and valuable employees retained.

I work for the Air Force. They have rewarded me well. Now I'm ready to apply all my passion for excellence to an organization like yours.

If I were in your shoes, I'd wonder why someone with such broad and deep experience would want to work for Apex. The reason is simple: Corinth is my home, and working here gives me an opportunity to add value to companies that are a lot closer to their customers than the large organizations found in bigger cities.

I've completed my online application. But, if my philosophy and track record appeal to you, I'd like to hear about Apex's GM needs in your own words. May I call in a few days to arrange time to do that?

Sincerely,

Ashley Meadows

Corinth, VT 05011
almeadows@hotmail.com
802-689-3490

- **It goes a step beyond the expected online application.** Ashley concludes by letting the reader know that she has completed the online application, as requested. But she has gone one step further by identifying the hiring manager and sending this letter. That initiative alone should serve to get her resume "pulled from the pile" (virtual or paper) and read by an actual human being.

Manuel Ramos Letter—Page 163

Manuel wants to work in a quasi-governmental or military organization, and his letter is an example of the second type of letter we mentioned in the early part of this section on military-to-civilian letters. Because Manuel is looking to stay closely aligned with the US Armed Forces, the letter showcases his specific skills and experience along with his record of service. Both of these are vital components for this particular job.

This letter starts with energy and enthusiasm, qualities that just about every employer embraces. It isn't hokey; it's sincere. Most importantly, it gives you a sense of the real person behind the resume. Bottom line, people hire people, so personality can make or break you in a job search. This letter demonstrates how to share a bit of *who* you are and engage the reader on a personal level.

The second paragraph, short and concise, addresses Manuel's military service, leadership, and other skills in strategic planning and business operations—all of which are essential for the advertised position.

Pay special attention to the 4 bulleted items, all of which relate to Federal Government contracting—professional certifications, cost savings, and other procurement-related achievements. These highlights illustrate what Manuel accomplished while on active duty and are precisely what the company will value most. The bullet format draws the eye to that most important information.

Mary Jones Letter—Page 164

The fourth military-to-civilian transition letter successfully addresses a big challenge: a total career change from military service managing helicopter maintenance to a new career in Accounting and Auditing.

Mary begins by sharing that she is currently pursuing both BS and MBA degrees with an emphasis in Accounting—strong academic credentials that qualify her for her new career. The first 3 paragraphs focus on her studies and academic performance, highlighted by a 4.0 grade point average (GPA) and other scholastic achievements. She even volunteered at tax season and received an "Awesome" review from the IRS!

The following paragraph addresses her prior experience in the US Army and then segues into the reason for her career change: She was wounded during her tour of duty in Iraq. She is not your typical military-to-civilian transition candidate. She has already left the military and is now attending college full-time after several years of recovery. Hers is a story of dedication and of excellence in work, school, and life.

Military Spouse and/or Volunteer

Military spouses often face 2 major obstacles to employment—a history of constant job changes, as the family has been stationed in multiple locations, and periods of unemployment and/or volunteer work. Yet both situations can easily be transformed into a strong presentation of qualifications.

From: **Manuel F. Ramos,** manuelramos@gmail.com
Subject: **Program Administrator Position**
Date: June 21, 2017
To: **J.K. Mottaghi,** jtmottaghi@mottaghicontractors.com

Dear Mr. Mottaghi:

I am eager to join forces with you as your new Program Administrator!

In addition to passion and motivation, I offer management experience in the Program Management sector, deep background in Government Contracting, well-honed strategic planning and business operations skills, and the well-recognized leadership qualities of a proud US Army veteran.

In addition, I would bring these key credentials and accomplishments to your organization:

- ➤ Earned the Federal Acquisition Certification for Program and Project Managers (FAC-P/PM).
- ➤ Awarded an Executive Certification in Government Contracts and Acquisition.
- ➤ Repurposed more than $100 million of a $1.4B portfolio.
- ➤ Saved more than $3 million in fees via a government-to-government procurement strategy.

In short, I have the skills, knowledge, and experience to be the liaison that your organization so much desires. I am very excited about this opportunity and believe that I would be a great fit for your team. May we schedule a meeting soon?

Sincerely,

Manuel Ramos
703-992-4451
manuelramos@gmail.com

MARY JONES

Atlanta Metro Area | 404-299-1212 | maryjones@gmail.com

January 23, 2017

Mr. Jerome Smith, Chief Financial Officer
Atlanta Accounting Associates
200 10th St.
Atlanta, GA 30309

Dear Mr. Smith:

I am extremely interested in exploring internship opportunities in your organization. As an **award-winning, 4.0 GPA MBA and BS student in Accounting** at the University of Georgia**,** I believe I have much to offer as I combine my strong record of professional successes, tenacity in pursuing goals, and enthusiasm for my new career in Accounting and Auditing.

I have completed most of the studies in my dual-degree program and expect to graduate in May 2017 with my BS and in 2018 with my MBA. Along the way, I have earned many honors and awards, including Dean's List, Chancellor's List, Beta Gamma Sigma International Honors Society membership, and several scholarships.

Based on my academic excellence, I was selected to coordinate and lead the IRS's Voluntary Tax Assistance effort on campus. I trained and led a 7-person team to successfully prepare more than 150 tax returns. Our efforts were described as **"Awesome!"** by the IRS.

Prior to changing my career goals, I served in the US Army, principally as an aircraft mechanic. I accelerated quickly through the ranks to become a Non-Commissioned Officer, achieving a leadership position within 2 years, as compared to the typical 8 years. I led a 6-person team to complete helicopter maintenance, troubleshooting, and repairs 40% faster than their peers.

Unfortunately, while deployed overseas, I was injured. After several years in recovery, I overcame all odds and now I am healthy. As I recovered, I reconsidered my goals and discovered a new passion—**auditing and accounting.** I love the exactitude of numbers, just as I loved the precision and attention to detail needed to maintain military aircraft at peak performance under high-stress situations.

I hope this brief synopsis helps you to understand the value I offer as an intern: current high-level knowledge, perseverance, attention to detail, eagerness to learn, and capacity for hard work.

Additional capabilities are listed in the attached resume. I will call your office within the next few days to see if we might set up a time to meet. If you have any questions, I can be reached at the number listed above. Thank you.

Sincerely,

Mary Jones

Resume attached

Robin Schlinger, MCD, CMRW, CFRW, CPRW, CECC, JCTC • Robin Resumes • robinresumes.com

Lucy Pine Letter—Page 166

Lucy's letter illustrates how to overcome both challenges to write a letter that showcases solid skills and experience—developed *because* of her life experiences holding many jobs and moving frequently as a military spouse.

Fortunately, Lucy is applying for a position working with the military, so the constant changes in her career aren't significant. In fact, her history actually makes her *more* qualified for the position of Social Services Assistant for a company that works with military service members and their families.

Key points in Lucy's letter:

- **Clarity.** Lucy starts by sharing that she is a military spouse—information that she knows will carry weight with the company to which she is applying..

- **Connection.** Lucy is very transparent that much of her experience comes from volunteering with various organizations that provide services to military families. By doing so, she makes another important connection between herself, the company, and the clients that it serves.

- **Relevance.** The 4 bulleted items bring attention to specific experiences Lucy has had—volunteer and paid—that match the requirements for the job. She strengthens her candidacy by writing about working directly with military families, serving on a steering committee to set strategy, helping to outline Command goals and career initiatives, and training others in military lifestyle.

- **Confidence.** The letter closes with a strong restatement of qualifications and a request for a personal interview. Lucy knows that she is qualified and assumes that she will be interviewed—and why not? She has precisely the qualifications that will make her a great employee.

Ex-Offenders

Regaining employment after incarceration is a challenge that affects hundreds of thousands of people every year. A key question is, when should you disclose the fact that you are an ex-offender?

In the vast majority of cases, we recommend that you **NOT disclose your incarceration in your letter or your resume.** Your goal is to get the interview and impress the interviewer, and most often the best way to do that is to maximize your skills and experience without mentioning that you have been in prison.

At some point—ideally at the end of the interview, after you have impressed the hiring manager with all that you know and all you can do—you will need to disclose your record. That can be a difficult conversation, so you should decide how best to explain things and then practice, practice, practice so you are confident during the interview.

Jason Baso Letter—Page 167

Jason's letter shows how to maximize skills and experience without ever mentioning prison. Similar to the letters in all other chapters of this book, Jason's message is all about his value and capabilities and how they relate to the employer's needs.

LUCY PINE

Everett, WA 98203 • 462.358.9742 • lpine@yahoo.com

SOCIAL SERVICES PROFESSIONAL

May 3, 2017

Lauren Scott
Executive Director
Dynamic Family Operations
Seattle, WA 98222

Dear Ms. Scott:

I am submitting my application for the **Social Services Assistant** position with your organization because, as a military spouse myself and an active volunteer, I have worked with military professionals in all stages of transition and believe that I can make a difference.

A few highlights that qualify me for this position are as follows:

- I was selected to serve as the Senior Advisor representing military families at the local base's community support meeting. As part of the Executive Steering Committee, I interfaced with leadership to discuss family concerns, including transition.

- As the Family Readiness Leader, I helped to outline Command goals and care initiatives. Confidentiality was an essential element in supporting families, especially during deployment.

- In another position, I increased marketing strategies for a local restaurant and boosted sales 25% and employee satisfaction 40%. This shows the ability to turn around an organization and make it flourish, despite a challenging past.

- Finally, I have developed and delivered key skill-building classes as a Military Trainer focused on resiliency within the military lifestyle, becoming an expert at teaching alternate ways for handling unpredictability.

Ms. Scott, I am an excellent candidate for the Social Services Assistant position because I have in-depth military knowledge, understand the relevant needs, and will work tirelessly to help military members transition successfully.

My resume can provide only an overview of my skills and qualifications—I hope to have the opportunity to share more details with you in person, and I will call on Monday to schedule an interview. Thank you.

Sincerely,

Lucy Pine

Attachment: Resume

Sophia Marshall, MHR, ACRW, BCC • Me Sheet • www.mesheet.com

From: **Jason Baso,** jason.baso@email.com
Subject: **Heavy Equipment Operator**
Date: March 9, 2017
To: **Eileen Markham,** eileen.markham@rylandhomes.com

Dear Ms. Markham:

In your search for a Heavy Equipment Operator, you will find my qualifications of interest:

- Hands-on experience operating **forklifts, tractors, loaders, backhoes, motor graders, track loaders, bulldozers, bobcat skid/steer loaders,** and **scrapers.**

- Certification as a **Heavy Equipment Operator** through Linn State Technical College.

- Ability to read and interpret **technical documents, drawings, maintenance manuals,** and **repair instructions.**

My work-related skills are solid, and I have clearly demonstrated that I can work independently, productively, and efficiently.

The opportunity to work for Ryland Homes is exciting, and I am most interested in meeting with you as soon as your schedule allows. I will call Tuesday morning, March 14, so that we can coordinate a specific date and time for an interview.

Thank you for your time and your consideration. I guarantee it will be worth it.

Sincerely,

Jason P. Baso
816-556-4567
jason.baso@email.com

Resume attached

Wendy Enelow, MRW, CCM, JCTC, CPRW • Enelow Executive Career Services • www.wendyenelow.com

Compare Jason's letter to the next 2 letters for ex-offenders in which both disclosed that they were in prison. This is highly unusual yet, in both of these circumstances, it was exactly the right thing to do. Let's look at them more closely.

William Smithe Letter—Page 169

William's letter is written to Mothers Against Drunk Drivers (MADD) for an internship opportunity. Yet William is not your typical intern or graduating student because 12 years ago he drove drunk, killed his best friend, and served 8 years in prison for his actions. He was also paralyzed in that crash.

William announces his history boldly at the very beginning of his letter and references it throughout the entire document. The story is sad, but it is also inspirational. The guilt he feels, the price he paid, and what he has done with his life while incarcerated all make a compelling case for William's candidacy. We would venture to guess that William got an interview and, most likely, an internship.

Patrick Martin Letter—Page 170

Patrick was a US Congressman before he went to prison for political "misdoings." He cannot hide that in his job search because his name is well known from all of the media coverage over the years. The very best thing in this situation is to "own it," as he does.

Patrick is realistic and knows that he will never again hold political office and, in fact, will not be working as an executive any time soon. His sights are set on a field sales position, and the content of the letter makes a great case for why he is so well qualified for the position. Lots of companies are going to turn Patrick away, others will interview him out of curiosity, and one or more will offer him a position because they know he can produce results.

> **Pro Tip: There are no rules to writing letters, resumes, LinkedIn profiles, or any other career communications.** Whether you disclose your incarceration in your letter will depend entirely on your specific situation and the company you are contacting.

As you know, incarceration is one of the most difficult obstacles to overcome in job search. Yet many more companies than you would expect are well known for their commitment to reintegrating ex-offenders into the workforce. Many of these companies are in the manufacturing, distribution, logistics, and transportation industries, but they are everywhere.

For the vast majority of ex-offenders, reaching out to recruiters will not be an effective job search strategy. Unless you have unusual and remarkably valuable skills and experience, recruiters generally will not present you to their client companies.

Spend time researching to identify the right companies for you, share a great resume and letter, and, during the interview, make them want to hire you so badly that incarceration is an afterthought … or, at the very least, not the first thought!

WILLIAM SMITHE

(406) 123-4567 | Wsmith1@gmail.com

January 1, 2017

Ms. Ruth Wadsworth, Human Resource Director
Mothers Against Drunk Driving (MADD)
511 E. John Carpenter Freeway, Suite 700
Irving, Texas 75062

Dear Ms. Wadsworth:

Twelve years ago, I made the worst mistake of my life . . . **I DROVE DRUNK AND KILLED MY BEST FRIEND.** The judge sentenced me to eight years in prison, two years of probation, and one year of counseling, while I sentenced myself to a lifetime in a wheelchair. Four years ago, I successfully completed my sentence and am proud to be graduating from college in June with a Family Communications Degree and Substance Abuse Counseling Certificate.

Since that dark night years ago, I have tried every day to make my friend's voice be heard and my life count. When I noticed a poster advertising your summer outreach program internship, I knew I had to apply.

Last fall, in partnership with the Missoula Family YMCA, I volunteered to help implement a grant-funded community awareness and youth education program specifically related to underage drinking and driving. I found the work meaningful, the messages impactful, and the training key to strengthening my skills in program design and implementation, parent workshop and student presentation facilitation, and volunteer recruitment and training.

I would like to continue to contribute to building safer communities, yet on a larger scale, by reaching broader targeted audiences through your outreach program.

I will forever live my life for two people, and if my (our) story could stop just one person from underage drinking and driving, I would gladly, repeatedly, and loudly tell it. If you seek an intern fully committed to and passionate about supporting the urgency of your mission, I would love to meet with you.

Sincerely,

William Smithe

Attachment: Resume

From: **Patrick Martin,** patrick@patrickmartin.com
Subject: **Referred by Angela Santos**
Date: April 6, 2017
To: **Charles Moran,** charlesmoran@arista.com

Dear Mr. Moran:

I would like to make it as easy as possible for Arista to add me to your team as your newest sales representative. First, before we go further, I want to address a concern you may have.

You likely have seen my name in the news, as I recently completed a prison sentence. I would understand if you stopped reading this letter right now. However, I hope you won't for several reasons that could benefit you and your firm.

I was a successful business founder and owner for several years. I've held positions from executive director to legislative assistant to US Congressman. As you might imagine, I've had a lot of time to think about my future.

I am blessed with the support of my exceptional family, my church, and the Centerville community. I am ready not just to make a new start, but to prove my worth. Therefore, I hold myself to standards much higher than most.

That's what drove me to tailor my resume to your needs. Right at the top are four profit-building capabilities you'll see me demonstrate from the first day on the job. Backing them up are 10 documented examples of increased revenue, stronger market share, and lower costs.

My job titles didn't have the word "sales" in them, but I was most definitely in that profession. I had to sell intangible ideas that drove the future of companies and communities. My "customers" were among the most demanding and sophisticated, and that experience gives me insights into selling that others may not have.

May I get on your schedule soon to explore how I might help remove any obstacles that stand between your sales goals and your monthly revenue?

Sincerely,

Patrick D. Martin
patrick@patrickmartin.com
Centerville, OH
216.888.0283 (cell)

LGBTQ Individuals

Sexual orientation or gender identity is very personal information, and there is almost never the need to share it. However, as mentioned, there are no rules to writing letters or resumes. The only "rule" is to write a letter that captures the reader's interest and connects you to their company or organization.

Denise Morningstar Letter—Page 172

Denise's letter illustrates when and why it is beneficial to share this personal information.

Denise is writing to a health care organization that is well known for its support of the LGBTQ community. She acknowledges their efforts and commitment and then, right in the first paragraph, writes *I'm proud that you are a part of my community.* That is all that needs to be said. Message received.

The rest of her letter very effectively showcases her professional skills and technical qualifications for the advertised position—Network Administrator. The letter closes with a short paragraph highlighting her soft skills and expressing her interest in interviewing for the position.

Denise's letter makes a connection with the company and the community it serves and is a great example of when unique and personal items can be used to a job seeker's advantage. There are many other times, beyond the LGBTQ community, when a similar strategy can be deployed to communicate that the job seeker is a part of, contributor to, or otherwise involved with a cause or community that has meaning or relevance to the employer.

Immigrants

Everyone has a story to tell, and sometimes that story can be the basis for a thoughtful letter that leaves a lasting impact. And isn't that the goal of a job search letter … to capture attention and move the reader to action?

Among the many challenges that immigrants face, finding appropriate employment can be one of the steepest. Credentials, skills, and experience from one country may not translate well nor be as highly valued in the new country, and immigrants often do not land jobs in the same profession nor at the same level as they held previously.

Given these circumstances, simply focusing on your skills, experiences, educational and professional credentials, achievements, and other qualifications may not be the only approach for your job search letters. Sometimes, your personal story will have more meaning and impact.

Kiran Chalise Letter—Page 173

Kiran's job search letter does not focus on his 15-year career as a finance and banking professional in Nepal. That information is included, but the letter is unusual in several aspects:

- **Personal Information.** Kiran begins by sharing the story and pathway of his family's recent immigration to the US. Most importantly, he tells the reader that he has a green card so is eligible to

DENISE MORNINGSTAR

Framingham, MA 01701 ◆ dmaltoso@gmail.com ◆ 508-879-7221

March 5, 2017

Fred Hovaginian, IT Director
Landmark Health
222 Massachusetts Avenue
Boston, MA 02115

Dear Mr. Hovaginian:

Landmark Health has always been recognized for cutting-edge initiatives, providing a safe place for people of diverse sexual orientations and gender identities to obtain critical medical, health, and wellness services. Congratulations on your 45th anniversary of service to the LGBTQ community! I'm proud that you are part of my community and am excited to submit my resume for the **Network Administrator** position.

My background in technology has exposed me to a variety of systems and project implementations, including networks, help desk, technical support, field support, and telephone voicemail management. My key contributions include:

- Infrastructure development and expansion to support increased users.
- Implementation and support for a Google Apps platform, virtual servers, and wireless technology.
- Upgrades and implementation of cutting-edge technologies—achieving a Bronze Metal for region-wide implementation of Local and Wide Area Networks.

I take great pride in my work, have a natural ability to listen to people's needs and frustrations, and create calm and confidence through comprehensive follow-through. I am confident that I can provide the level and quality of technical support that your organization needs and deserves. I look forward to the opportunity to interview for this position and will follow up with you if I don't hear back within a few days. Thank you.

Best regards,

Denise Morningstar

Stephanie Legatos, CPRW • Visible You • visibleyou.biz

Kiran Chalise

Savannah, GA • KiranChalise@yahoo.com • 912-878-1888

May 16, 2017

David Brown
Director of Human Resources
UBS International
400 Colony Square, Suite 410
Atlanta, GA 30326

Dear Mr. Brown:

I, along with my wife and 4-year-old daughter, have recently arrived in America. It is an honor to be in this great country. We were provided green cards and a pathway to citizenship as part of a program administered by the US Department of State (DOS), through the US Embassy in our country of Nepal.

The Diversity Immigrant Visa Program selects applicants from countries with low rates of immigration to the United States. All selected applicants are carefully screened to ensure they meet essential education and work experience requirements. In Nepal, education is highly valued and considered of the utmost importance.

I am looking forward to opportunities in America, as I am well educated and have a great deal of professional experience. I have a Master's Degree in Finance and have spent 15 years in the banking industry in Nepal, as you will note in my attached resume. Also, please know that I am very willing to start at an entry-level position.

While I know that skills and experience are critical, I also bring other strengths for which I have been recognized:

➢ Commitment and dedication to excellence, as evidenced by numerous promotions and letters of appreciation from colleagues and our CEO.

➢ Outstanding leadership and teamwork skills, demonstrated by consistently exceeding customer acquisition goals by 200% or more.

➢ Practical experience from 15 years in the banking industry, a dedicated work ethic, and, according to peers and managers, strong interpersonal skills and a "friendly nature."

Based on my experience and personal strengths, I feel confident that I could be a positive contributor to the success of UBS. I have also taken the liberty of including a Letter of Appreciation given to me from our CEO upon my departure to America. I hope to meet with you soon and will follow up with a call on Friday. Thank you.

Sincerely,

Kiran Chalise

Enclosure: Resume

work in the US. Green cards can be difficult to acquire and, by mentioning it early on in the letter, he instantly eliminates a potential roadblock.

- **Current Targets.** Next, Kiran concisely summaries his impressive educational credentials and 15 years of work experience. But he is realistic, knows that he is most likely not going to land a senior-level position after only a few months in the US, and states that he is willing to start at the bottom to prove his worth. By so doing, he has positioned himself for both lower-level and higher-level opportunities. Perfect!

- **Value and Achievements.** Like many powerful job search letters, Kiran's letter includes bulleted items that highlight his professional skills, essential soft skills, and notable achievements, such as fast-track promotion and very strong performance in sales and customer management.

- **Third-Party Reference.** The closing paragraph mentions an enclosed letter of recommendation, an unusual thing to share so early in the job search process but very valuable in this unique situation. Third-party validation of his performance adds great value to his candidacy.

Not every immigrant will need to share such a personal story to get an employer's attention. Think first about your skills and qualifications and how those relate to an employer's needs. Then consider whether it will be beneficial to share a deeper background to help employers understand your value.

If so, your letter, like Kiran's, should combine the *personal* with the *professional*. A compelling story enhances your skills, but you still must appeal to the employer's bottom-line needs.

CHAPTER 9:
Job Proposal Letters

What is a Job Proposal Letter?

A job proposal letter is one of a kind, written to make a case for _you_ as the solution to a very specific business problem or challenge. Written immediately after an interview, it is a letter/proposal that puts forth a persuasive business argument for precisely what you will bring to the organization.

Do not confuse job proposal letters with thank-you letters that you will _always_ send after an interview, as we discussed in Chapter 7. A job proposal letter serves an entirely different function, as you will learn in this chapter.

Job proposal letters, which you will use much less frequently than thank-you letters, should be written only in unique circumstances, such as the following:

- **The company has communicated that there are several well-qualified candidates** and you want to share why you are the best candidate with the most valuable talent and experience.

- **The company has not made a firm commitment to filling the position under consideration** because of strategic, operational, financial, or other considerations.

- **The company expressed some concerns regarding your candidacy** and you want to dispel those concerns and offer overwhelming evidence for why the company should extend the offer to you.

- **The company has not firmly defined the position** and you want to provide clarity in terms of the requisite talents needed and, of course, the fact that you alone possess the unique skill set for reaching the company's desired goals.

> **Pro Tip:** Write job proposal letters that clearly communicate why the company should hire you and what value you will deliver to the organization. These letters share detailed information that will resonate with that particular company and convince them that they cannot take the risk of _not_ hiring you.

One additional circumstance for writing a job proposal letter is when you are already employed by the company but you have identified an opportunity where you can add even more value. To address this opportunity, you might propose an expansion of your job duties or the creation of a new, higher level position. You will find an example of this type of job proposal letter on page 179.

What Do You Want to Achieve in Your Job Proposal Letter?

Your job proposal needs to make a compelling business case, one that the company would be foolish to ignore! To do that, you must have a clear understanding of the employer's needs and challenges and demonstrate how hiring you will bring more value than cost.

Bottom line, you want to communicate that hiring you—for an existing or a new position—will provide the company with the talent they must have to meet specific operational and/or financial goals.

How Do You Write a Job Proposal Letter?

A job proposal letter is "just the facts" more than any other type of career marketing message. You have gathered the details during your interview(s) with the company—you know the specific problems or challenges they are facing, and your job proposal spells out how you are the solution.

In your letter, reiterate the facts of the business case, specifically:

- **The problem or situation the company is facing** and the immediate and long-term impact.

- **The cost to the company of not resolving this problem.** Cost might include actual cash losses or perhaps opportunity costs, competitive slippage, market-share losses, or other negative impacts. Use specific numbers whenever possible.

- **What you propose to do about it**—how your expertise will solve the problem.

- **The value you will deliver with your solution.** Be specific about the financial, operational, technological, product, and other benefits the company will gain from hiring you.

Your job proposal letter will not look or read like any other letters you will write during your job search. For one thing, as mentioned, it must be written specifically to *one* company offering *one* solution (you!) to a very precisely defined problem.

Also, it might be structured more as a proposal than as a standard letter—with clear delineation of problems, proposed solutions, costs, and benefits. Look at the sample job proposal letters in this chapter and you will clearly see how different they can be in their construction and presentation.

How Do You Submit a Job Proposal Letter?

More often than not, you will email your job proposal letters as attached Word or PDF files. Throughout most of this book, we have recommended that your letters should be e-notes—the actual email messages. However, in this situation, when the letter will most likely be longer and more detailed than other types of job search letters, we recommend that you make it a more formal presentation. Introduce your letter with a brief email message that refers to your attached job proposal letter.

> **Pro Tip: Send your job proposal letters on nicely formatted letterhead to transmit a professional document that is reflective of the quality of work that you will produce on behalf of that company.** Consider these letters as your first assignment for the company and show them what you can do.

Remember that job proposal letters are business proposals, and approach them precisely that way. The content, tone, and presentation should combine to communicate a well-written message of value, professionalism, and understanding of the business.

If you like solving business problems, you might find that you enjoy writing job proposal letters more than any others during your job search. In your letter you can make a clear and convincing case based on hard facts. You can focus on problem/solution and not feel like you have to "sell" yourself—rather, you are making an irresistible argument for what the company will gain by hiring you.

Who is the Audience?

The audience for your job proposal letters can vary widely based on who you interviewed with. That might include:

- Hiring Managers
- HR Associates, Managers & Directors
- Prospective Colleagues
- Directors & C-Level Executives
- Presidents, Executive Vice Presidents & Vice Presidents
- Chairmen of the Board & Board Directors
- Venture Capitalists & Private Equity Investors

Always keep in mind that you want to send these letters to decision makers and to people who can influence someone else's decision to make you an offer.

To Whom Do You Send It?

Send your job proposal letter to the person or people that you interviewed with as a detailed follow-up immediately after your interview.

Unlike thank-you letters, which need to be customized if you interviewed with multiple people, you can send the exact same job proposal letter to every one of those individuals. In fact, you *should* send the same letter, since you are proposing one particular job based on that company's specific needs.

What are the Unique Characteristics of a Job Proposal Letter?

To best understand the nuances of the job proposal letters that follow in this chapter, be certain to read the box at the bottom of every letter. The boxes include specifics about each letter—the situation behind the letter, why it was written in the way that it was, and important points that you should pay attention to within that specific proposal.

DAVID GONZALEZ

New Haven, CT 06514 ♦ (203) 555-4567 ♦ david.gonzalez@mac.com ♦ linkedin.com/in/davidgonzalez

Date: May 12, 2017
To: Angelina Pepe
From: David Gonzalez
Re: **Proposal for Project Cost Analyst: Pepe Consulting Group**

Thank you for your time on Monday. It was a genuine pleasure to meet you and explore the challenges and opportunities you face as you continue to grow Pepe Consulting into a regional powerhouse! It would be exciting for me to join your team … and, I believe, very valuable to you to add my skills as described in this proposal.

POSITION: Project Cost Analyst

PROBLEM SOLVED: Better understanding the true costs of each project engagement. Your current proposal process is rather "hit or miss," in that you don't fully understand the real costs of executing each project. Without this vital information, you risk:

- Underbidding project proposals, thereby making them unprofitable.
- Overbidding project proposals, thereby making them uncompetitive.
- Underspending on critical aspects of project management.
- Overspending on unnecessary project components.

VALUE DELIVERED: Project cost control and accurate data for immediate and long-term benefit. I would begin by analyzing all projects proposed and delivered in the past year to gain an accurate understanding of estimated and actual costs. From these benchmarks we can fine-tune the proposal process to more accurately reflect costs and ensure that proposals are both profitable and competitive.

Ongoing, the data will allow us to track the profitability of each project and compare to norms, so that we know when—and can investigate why—a project comes in widely outside average ranges. If it's more costly … we need to know why and prevent it from happening again. If it's more profitable … again we need to know why and see how we can apply those factors to all projects to increase the firm's profits overall.

COST–BENEFIT ANALYSIS: Based on a review of 3 of your recent projects and a comparison with industry averages, I estimate that Pepe Consulting is losing at least 5% per project through overspending or underbidding. Therefore, on $4M in project revenue annually, the conservative estimate is that I could generate an additional $200,000 in project revenue and/or cost reduction through a dedicated effort to project cost analysis.

PROPOSAL:

- Creation of new position of Project Cost Analyst—a position I am highly qualified to fill based on my 4 years of Cost Accounting experience, 3 years in Project Management, BS in Business, and strong analytical skills.
- Salary of $95,000 per year and performance bonus of 15% of all financial gains (revenue increases or cost reductions) above $200,000 that can be directly tied to my efforts.
- Review after 1 year with position refinement and compensation increase based on value delivered.

SUMMARY: Confident of my ability to generate both immediate and long-lasting benefits for Pepe Consulting, I look forward to discussing this proposal and—hopefully—joining your team to help each project, and the company overall, become more competitive, more profitable, and more dominant in the region.

> After an introductory meeting in which the business owner was very candid about her challenge of identifying the cost of consulting engagements, this job seeker developed a proposal that is very easy for her to accept: The cost of hiring him will be less than the projected benefits, and the initial commitment is for just 1 year.

Louise Kursmark, MRW, CPRW, CCM, JCTC, CEIP • Best Impression Career Services • www.louisekursmark.com

JORDAN L. MONTGOMERY

☎ 336.123.4567 | 🖳 jlmontg#01@yahoo.com

16 Jun 2017

TO: Mr. John Rawlings, Chief – Training Division
Training Solutions, Inc.

SUBJECT: INCREASED JOB ROLES/RESPONSIBILITIES PROPOSAL

OVERVIEW

As **WORKFORCE DEVELOPMENT PROGRAM MANAGER**, my primary roles and responsibilities are to:

- Submit requests for bids to contractors interested in conducting on- and off-site computer-based training.
- Conduct site visits to evaluate capability/efficiency of both instructors and instructional methodologies.
- Review end-of-course surveys and make recommendations.

CASE STUDY/FINDINGS

Based on my own initiative after attending a position-specific training session facilitated by a contractor, I discovered that despite our agency paying for a full week of training, students were receiving only three days of quantifiable qualitative training. I shared my findings during a roundtable "think-tank" session designed to identify contractor/attendee issues, exchange views on procedural shortfalls, analyze current operatives, and determine/ reexamine short- and long-term goals with designated internal business leaders.

Invited to take my findings to the next level, I propose this solution: enhancement/elevation of my current role.

PROPOSAL

Additional responsibility as **AUTOMATION TRAINING INSTRUCTIONAL STRATEGIST**:

- Plan, develop, and implement in-house computer-based training to replace existing outsourced service.
- Design instructor/student lesson plans with clearly defined learning objectives.
- Employ subject-matter expertise to create a comprehensive task analysis matrix documenting task mastery and measuring training effectiveness.

COST/BENEFIT ANALYSIS

- Increase my current annual salary by 20% ($15K).
- Current class sizes must have a minimum of seven students and be conducted on a biweekly basis, costing $150 per attendee. Total minimum monthly cost is $2,100 x 12 months equals $25,200.
- Bringing training in-house will result in a first-year savings for the organization of $10,200—while also improving student tracking, measuring student learning, and increasing subject mastery.

An example of a proposition to increase job duties (and salary) by an existing employee, this job proposal letter makes a strong argument based on a case study and analysis of existing practices. Note the "Cost/Benefit Analysis" showing value delivered of more than $10,000 in the first year alone!

Phyllis Houston • The Resume Expert • http://www.rezxprt.com

From: **Selena Martin,** selena.martin@SCMConsulting.com
Subject: **Proposal for your consideration** … Follow-up to Friday's phone call
Date: June 9, 2017
To: **Pamela Givens,** pgivens@videopartners.com

Pam, as promised, I am pleased to provide this proposal and look forward to further discussion.

Proposed Job Title: Relationship Manager, Megamart Account
Reporting to: Pamela Givens, Director of Sales & Marketing

Job Scope: Key to the success of the In-Store Broadcasting Network debut at Megamart, the Relationship Manager position requires someone who can do the following:

- Build and manage relationships at the executive level within Megamart and with key program sponsors to ensure smooth implementation and customer satisfaction.

- Serve as an expert resource to the In-Store Broadcasting Network sales team, introducing advertisers to the concept, value, benefits, and long-term growth opportunities of narrowcasting.

- Help shape and design the day-to-day workflow to launch and operate the network, ensuring a product that is easy to use and thus driving positive customer reaction to the new experience.

Job Significance: The critical nature of the Megamart business cannot be overstated. The success of this initiative will be the stepping stone to other retailers and will establish the company as an industry leader. And because it is a major initiative in a new media for Megamart, its value must be proven—immediately. "Getting it right the first time" is a must.

For Megamart, there are significant dangers that can result from poor execution by the Relationship Manager: A faulty startup or poor programming can mean damaged relationships, advertiser dissatisfaction, loss of market share, and other long-term repercussions.

Selena Martin Expertise/Compensation Proposal: We have agreed that I possess the right blend of skills and expertise for this position. In brief, I offer:

- Unparalleled expertise in the emerging narrowcasting industry
- Extensive range of industry contacts
- Executive-level relationship management skills
- Marketing and advertising savvy
- Project management skills and detail orientation

I anticipate a compensation package that reflects the significance of the position and includes appropriate performance bonuses based on predetermined areas of strategic importance. Specifically:

- Base salary between $110,000–$135,000
- Performance bonus based on predefined benchmarks for project tollgates, deliverables, timetables, and eventual rollout
- Standard package of company benefits

Pam, I know you want to move forward quickly to fill this position in advance of kick-off meetings. I too am eager to get started. I would be happy to discuss this proposal in more detail at your convenience.

Selena Martin
SCM Consulting • 414-234-1615

> After a young company landed a major contract to provide in-store broadcasting technology, they brought in a consultant … and realized that a full-time person was needed to lead the important program. The consultant developed this e-note proposal, based on her knowledge of the company, its technology, and the client.

Louise Kursmark, MRW, CPRW, CCM, JCTC, CEIP • Best Impression Career Services • www.louisekursmark.com

Jeff Weismann

JeffWeismann@gmail.com   917.555.1212

June 21, 2017

Jane Reiss
CEO, Alston Consulting
1547 Springfield Avenue
Morristown, NJ 07113

Dear Jane:

Thank you for your time this week. Based on our discussions, I've created a job proposal designed to answer many of Alston Consulting's needs. I look forward to reviewing the proposal with you and adjusting it to fit your vision for the **Program Services and Strategy Director** position.

As a growing business consulting organization for small to medium-sized businesses (SMBs), Alston Consulting needs the agility to respond to real-time changes in the market so that every aspect of the firm is current on business trends. Client-facing resources must reflect that same level of integrity with industry-specific materials that serve clients' specific needs.

Adding the **Program Services and Strategy Director** position to Alston's team will result in swift and long-term solutions. Here are 5 initiatives I will fully develop, launch, and manage that are on point with Alston's goals, as we discussed:

1) **Professional Development for Staff Consultants:** Conduct monthly 1-hour classes delivered live via video that will expand the expertise of the nationwide team. Topics identified as immediate needs include partnering with SMB leadership, developing growth strategies for SMBs, and managing clients' digital dirt.

2) **Resources for Clients:** Build Alston's library from its current limited state into one that is robust and regarded as a go-to resource by clients. First up on the deliverables will be SMB branding and advertising, followed by cash flow management, customer service in the digital age, and market share development.

3) **Thought Leadership:** Position Alston as a thought leader in the industry by publishing research studies and hosting conferences that simultaneously spotlight research and promote industry best practices.

4) **Technology:** Introduce 3 key technology solutions to advance Alston's capabilities and efficiencies. These solutions include *accounting software* for enabling automatic billing, payments, and contract renewals; *video software* for building a stronger, more personalized internal culture among nationwide team members; and a *cloud office system* that combines the ease and familiarity of social media with a more high-tech, secure approach to file sharing, meeting planning, and project management.

5) **Program Planning:** Develop structured, scalable programs that respond to clients' expressed needs for succession planning, international expansion, staff development, regulatory compliance, and product development.

With adoption of this proposal and me in the **Program Services and Strategy Director** position, Alston will reach the next level in this industry. We'll be sure to build out each initiative with Alston's corporate culture, budget, and bandwidth in mind to ensure efforts are realistic and successful. And we will attach specific deadlines and milestones to the initiatives.

Jane, throughout our conversations, I've been impressed by Alston Consulting's accomplishments. I am excited to continue that path of success with these proposed ideas. Thank you for your consideration.

Sincerely,

Jeff Weismann
Certified Program Services Professional

> The highlights of this job proposal letter are the 5 specific programs that the job seeker promises to "fully develop, launch, and manage"—programs that advance the company's goals, align with its corporate culture, and call for the precise expertise that this job seeker offers.

Kimberly Schneiderman, CLTMC, NCRW, CEIC • RiseSmart • www.risesmart.com

DANA RHODES

Proposed Role: Vice President, Corporate Technology—Southwest Payment Systems   *May 17, 2017*

Your Challenges:

As the leading global provider of merchant processing services, Southwest Payment Systems provides sophisticated technical services to a diversified customer base. Its internal IT capability is currently straining to remain strategic, current, and valued by its internal customers.

At this point it is critical to introduce a more strategic perspective to internal IT planning and service delivery. Otherwise, while the business will continue to grow and invest in IT, its systems will not address the long-term objectives of the company and may not necessarily be the best use of resources.

A worst-case scenario would be to combine stop-gap or band-aid measures with ambitious new initiatives that are costly, time-consuming, and laden with promise but not ultimately the best solution for the company's present and future needs.

My Value:

My strongest expertise is in strategic planning and streamlined delivery of IT solutions that deliver the greatest value to users while aligning with the mission of the organization. Thus, I am an excellent adjunct to the current EVP to meet the rapidly evolving needs of internal customers and elevate the internal IT organization to a world-class level commensurate with the size, success, and promise of the organization.

Proposed Solution

- Strategically manage IT resources to support the company's rapid growth and ensure the delivery of best-in-class technology and tools to a diverse user base.

- Develop strategic technology plans that support both immediate needs and long-term business goals.

- Create a nimble IT organization that can readily respond to changes, challenges, and growth.

- Sharpen performance of the IT department by instilling a project management focus and improving quality, reliability, productivity, and customer focus.

- Reduce conflict and strengthen internal communications by translating technical terms, concepts, and projects into everyday business language that is clearly understood by people throughout the organization.

I am very keen to further explore this proposal with you and share additional details about how I can strengthen the IT organization, reduce executive time and effort currently spent managing internal IT issues, and add value to the company.

DANA RHODES
Dana.Rhodes@gmail.com • 617-345-6789

> Sent as an attachment via email, this job proposal letter is a standalone document that can easily be shared with other decision makers. It clearly defines the challenges and presents the job seeker as the ideal solution.

Louise Kursmark, MRW, CPRW, CCM, JCTC, CEIP • Best Impression Career Services • www.louisekursmark.com

Appendix

The Appendix provides 2 very useful tools to help you write more powerful, descriptive, specific, and effective job search letters:

- List of 426 Resume Writing Verbs
- List of 221 Personality Descriptors

Browse the lists when you need ideas or inspiration to find just the right word for your cover letter or e-note. You'll also find them helpful as you are writing your resume, LinkedIn profile, and other career communications.

426 Resume Writing Verbs

Accelerate	Architect	Captain	Compile	Corroborate
Accentuate	Arrange	Capture	Complete	Counsel
Accomplish	Articulate	Catalog	Comply	Craft
Accommodate	Ascertain	Catapult	Compute	Create
Achieve	Assemble	Centralize	Conceive	Critique
Acquire	Assess	Champion	Conceptualize	Crystallize
Adapt	Assist	Change	Conclude	Curtail
Address	Attain	Chart	Conduct	Cut
Adjudicate	Augment	Clarify	Configure	Decipher
Administer	Authenticate	Classify	Conserve	Decrease
Advance	Author	Close	Consolidate	Define
Advise	Authorize	Coach	Construct	Delegate
Advocate	Balance	Cobble	Consult	Deliver
Align	Believe	Collaborate	Contemporize	Demonstrate
Alter	Bestow	Collect	Continue	Deploy
Analyze	Brainstorm	Command	Contract	Derive
Anchor	Brief	Commercialize	Control	Design
Apply	Budget	Commoditize	Convert	Detail
Appoint	Build	Communicate	Convey	Detect
Appreciate	Calculate	Compare	Coordinate	Determine
Arbitrate	Capitalize	Compel	Correct	Develop

Devise	Ensure	Guide	Leverage	Optimize
Differentiate	Entrench	Halt	Liaise	Orchestrate
Diminish	Equalize	Handle	License	Order
Direct	Eradicate	Head	Listen	Organize
Discard	Espouse	Helmed	Locate	Orient
Discern	Establish	Hire	Lower	Originate
Discover	Estimate	Honor	Maintain	Outpace
Dispense	Evaluate	Hypothesize	Manage	Outperform
Display	Examine	Identify	Manipulate	Outsource
Distinguish	Exceed	Illustrate	Manufacture	Overcome
Distribute	Excel	Imagine	Map	Overhaul
Diversify	Execute	Implement	Market	Oversee
Divert	Exhibit	Import	Marshal	Participate
Document	Exhort	Improve	Master	Partner
Dominate	Expand	Improvise	Mastermind	Perceive
Double	Expedite	Increase	Maximize	Perfect
Draft	Experiment	Influence	Measure	Perform
Drive	Explode	Inform	Mediate	Persuade
Earn	Explore	Initiate	Mentor	Pilot
Edit	Export	Innovate	Merge	Pinpoint
Educate	Extract	Inspect	Minimize	Pioneer
Effect	Extricate	Inspire	Model	Plan
Effectuate	Facilitate	Install	Moderate	Position
Elect	Finalize	Institute	Modify	Predict
Elevate	Finance	Instruct	Monetize	Prepare
Eliminate	Follow up	Integrate	Monitor	Prescribe
Emphasize	Forecast	Intensify	Motivate	Present
Empower	Forge	Interpret	Navigate	Preside
Enact	Form	Interview	Negotiate	Prevent
Encourage	Formalize	Introduce	Network	Process
Endeavor	Formulate	Invent	Nominate	Procure
Endorse	Foster	Inventory	Normalize	Produce
Endure	Found	Investigate	Obfuscate	Program
Energize	Fulfill	Judge	Obliterate	Progress
Enforce	Gain	Justify	Observe	Project
Engineer	Garner	Land	Obtain	Project manage
Enhance	Generate	Launch	Offer	Proliferate
Enlist	Govern	Lead	Officiate	Promote
Enliven	Graduate	Lecture	Operate	Propel

Propose	Redesign	Reuse	Standardize	Thwart
Prospect	Reduce	Review	Steer	Train
Prove	Reengineer	Revise	Stimulate	Transcribe
Provide	Regain	Revitalize	Strategize	Transfer
Publicize	Regulate	Salvage	Streamline	Transform
Purchase	Rehabilitate	Sanctify	Strengthen	Transition
Purify	Reimagine	Satisfy	Structure	Translate
Qualify	Reinforce	Save	Study	Trim
Quantify	Rejuvenate	Schedule	Substantiate	Troubleshoot
Query	Relate	Secure	Succeed	Uncover
Question	Remedy	Select	Suggest	Unify
Raise	Render	Separate	Summarize	Unite
Rate	Renegotiate	Serve	Supervise	Update
Ratify	Renew	Service	Supplement	Upgrade
Realign	Renovate	Set up	Supply	Use
Rebuild	Reorganize	Shepherd	Support	Utilize
Recapture	Report	Simplify	Surpass	Validate
Receive	Reposition	Slash	Synergize	Verbalize
Recognize	Represent	Sold	Synthesize	Verify
Recommend	Research	Solidify	Systematize	Win
Reconcile	Resolve	Solve	Tabulate	Work
Record	Respond	Spark	Tailor	Write
Recruit	Restore	Speak	Target	
Rectify	Restructure	Spearhead	Teach	
Recycle	Retain	Specialize	Terminate	
Redefine	Retrieve	Specify	Test	

Personality Descriptors—Soft Skills and Attributes

Abstract	Artful	Competent	Creative	Dedicated
Accurate	Assertive	Competitive	Credible	Dependable
Action-Driven	Believable	Conceptual	Cross-Cultural	Detail-Oriented
Adaptable	Bilingual	Confident	Culturally	Determined
Adventurous	Bold	Conscientious	Conscious	Devoted
Aggressive	Brave	Conservative	Culturally Sensitive	Diligent
Agile	Capable	Consistent	Customer-Driven	Diplomatic
Amenable	Collaborative	Cooperative	Dauntless	Direct
Analytical	Communicative	Courageous	Decisive	Dramatic

Driven	Impactful	Orderly	Quick Learner	Top Performer
Dynamic	Important	Organized	Reactive	Top Producer
Eager	Impressive	Outstanding	Reliable	Traditional
Earnest	Incomparable	Participative	Reputable	Trainer
Effective	Individualistic	Participatory	Resilient	Transformative
Efficient	Industrious	Passionate	Resourceful	Trilingual
Eloquent	Independent	Peerless	Respectful	Troubleshooter
Employee-Driven	Ingenious	Perfectionist	Responsive	Trustworthy
Empowered	Innovative	Performance-Driven	Results-Driven	Truthful
Encouraging	Insightful	Persevering	Results-Oriented	Unifying
Energetic	Intelligent	Persistent	Savvy	Unrelenting
Energized	Intense	Personable	Selfless	Understanding
Enterprising	Intuitive	Persuasive	Sensitive	Up-To-Date
Enthusiastic	Investigative	Philosophical	Sharp	Upbeat
Entrepreneurial	Judicious	Photogenic	Skilled	Valiant
Ethical	Keen	Pioneering	Skillful	Valuable
Experienced	Leader	Poised	Sophisticated	Venturesome
Expert	Loyal	Polished	Specialist	Veracious
Expressive	Managerial	Popular	Spirited	Verbal
Flexible	Market-Driven	Positive	Strategic	Victorious
Focused	Masterful	Practical	Strong	Vigorous
Forward-Thinking	Mature	Pragmatic	Subjective	Virtuous
Global	Mechanical	Precise	Successful	Visionary
Go-Getter	Methodical	Preeminent	Tactful	Vital
Hardworking	Mindful	Prepared	Tactical	Vivacious
Healthy	Modern	Proactive	Talented	Well-Balanced
Helpful	Moral	Problem-Solver	Task-Oriented	Well-Versed
Heroic	Motivated	Productive	Teacher	Winning
High-Impact	Motivational	Professional	Team Builder	Wise
High-Potential	Multilingual	Proficient	Team Leader	Worldly
Honest	Notable	Progressive	Team Player	Youthful
Honorable	Noteworthy	Prominent	Technical	Zealous
Humanistic	Objective	Prompt	Tenacious	Zestful
Humanitarian	Observant	Prudent	Thorough	
Humorous	Opportunistic	Punctual	Timely	
Immediate	Oratorical	Quality-Driven	Tolerant	

Job Search Letter Index

Following is one of the most valuable resources in the book—an index of all 125+ letters samples sliced and diced in countless ways. You can search by:

- **Industry or profession:** Samples for jobs you've held in the past or those you are now pursuing.
- **Circumstance:** Letters that have worked for those dealing with issues that put a wrinkle in the job search and letter development process—career change, military transition, incarceration, and more.

Use the index wisely to find the right letter samples to guide you in writing, formatting, and designing letters that work for you—that will help you *get noticed and get hired.*

Search by Industries and Professions

MANUFACTURING, OPERATIONS & TRANSPORTATION
Visit these pages for samples and ideas: 7, 13, 44, 48, 53, 74, 79, 87, 146, 156

NONPROFITS, ASSOCIATIONS & GOVERNMENT AGENCIES
Visit these pages for samples and ideas: 14, 38, 117, 145, 148, 157, 163, 166, 169

PERSONAL SERVICES
Visit these pages for samples and ideas: 48, 76

SALES, MARKETING, RETAIL & CUSTOMER SERVICE
Visit these pages for samples and ideas: 10, 32, 33, 35, 39, 40, 42, 49, 50, 51, 58, 63, 67, 68, 69, 72, 80, 81, 83, 84, 86, 91, 99, 100, 101, 114, 115, 116, 119, 120, 131, 132, 134, 140, 141, 142, 144, 147, 153, 154, 170, 180

SKILLED TRADES & CONSTRUCTION
Visit these pages for samples and ideas: 14, 64, 65, 73, 88, 130, 167

TEACHING & EDUCATION
Visit these pages for samples and ideas: 41, 75, 179

TECHNOLOGY & TELECOMMUNICATIONS
Visit these pages for samples and ideas: 14, 35, 36, 45, 46, 47, 56, 57, 68, 77, 78, 84, 85, 90, 91, 101, 116, 118, 119, 133, 143, 148, 149, 154, 172, 182

Search by Career Circumstance

CAREER CHANGE
Visit these pages for samples and ideas: 153, 154, 156, 157, 164, 170

MILITARY TRANSITION
Visit these pages for samples and ideas: 160, 161, 163, 164

MILITARY SPOUSE AND/OR VOLUNTEERISM
Visit these pages for samples and ideas: 166

INCARCERATION
Visit these pages for samples and ideas: 167, 169, 170

LGBTQ
Visit these pages for samples and ideas: 172

IMMIGRATION
Visit these pages for samples and ideas: 173